What did you do today
that brought you joy?®

FINANCIAL PLANNING MADE PERSONAL

How to Create Joy And The Mindset for Success

LAWRENCE SPRUNG, CFP®

mf
MITLIN FINANCIAL

ISBN: 979-8-218-23256-6

All proceeds from the sale of this book are being donated to the Keith Milano Memorial Fund at the American Foundation for Suicide Prevention.

Dedication

To Mitchell Fried and Linda Sprung.
the namesakes of Mitlin Financial,
who gave us the "Mit" and "Lin" in our firm's name
and whose legacy and inherent values live on
in our commitment to the families we serve.

Table of Contents

Foreword

It's fascinating how much the world can change in a few decades. And yet, how much some things stay the same.

I started my career as a financial advisor in 1983. Back then, rising interest rates and inflation were making their impact known across the country, much like they are 40 years later. As a young man who was raised on a farm in the early 1980s—and then saw his family go bankrupt because of the financial environment—I was determined to dedicate my career to helping others avoid the same financial ruin I saw firsthand with my parents.

On the flip side, unlike the 1980s, today we have countless tools, resources, and technology to enhance our financial lives, from budgeting tools that provide real-time transparency into our financial accounts to predictive analytics that can forecast any number of scenarios years or decades into the future. That's without mentioning any trailblazers in the markets today like cryptocurrency or the metaverse.

Our lives have grown more connected and also more complicated. We expect immediacy with every exchange and measure our experiences based on the convenience and clarity they deliver. However, even with these modern-day standards and ever-increasing expectations, individuals and families still aren't getting the financial advice they deserve.

I've considered myself fortunate to have built a 40-year career as a financial advisor and to see the way our profession has evolved to meet the needs of the families we serve. We have come a long way in helping others find their financial freedom since the days of ticker tape, but the expansive impact we can have has yet to be fully realized. We live in a world full of accelerating change, uncertainty, division, and confusion. This is especially true when it comes to our financial lives. We're starving for someone we can trust. Someone who will simplify our financial lives, take care of our assets just as they would their own, and anticipate our needs before we know we have them.

That's what we at Carson Group call delivering on the Third Level of Trust. Without elevating to this level of service for the families we serve, poor decisions are made, and financial freedom is lost.

Larry and I have known each other for many years, and we partnered with each other because we know what it takes to surprise and delight the families we serve. There is no better feeling in the world than knowing you've helped someone who never expected it and can never repay you. That's the level of impact we both want to have with the families we serve every day. That's the reason we jump out of bed in the morning, excited to take on a new day.

The reason Larry wrote this book—and the reason we decided to work together years ago—is because we both believe there is so much we are capable of doing in our role as financial advisors. Beyond the assets, the wealth, and the money lies a deeper purpose of helping others live out the life they envision. This is something I've always referred to as attaining True Wealth: all that money can't buy and death can't take away. If we can't help you identify what you value most, clarify how to prioritize your resources and energy to pursue those values, and then help you design a path to help get you there, we aren't doing our job as your advisor.

A long-held stigma still infiltrates the minds of the masses. It's the belief that financial planners only work with the wealthy. Nothing could be further from the truth, especially when it comes to the collective mission we share as advisors at Carson Group. My hope for you in reading this book is that it encourages you to think differently, informs you on how to take steps in your own financial life, and equips you with the discerning knowledge of what type of advisor is best matched for you.

Over the next several chapters, you'll see just how connected your personal habits and beliefs are to the goals you pursue in this life, financially or otherwise. Larry thoughtfully connects the dots, from reflecting on how you spend your time, to revealing best practices in living the life you desire, to protecting your assets that can then be used in limitless ways to live your life by design, not by default.

Every chapter concludes with practical advice and helpful questions, allowing you to produce a game plan for making your freedom a reality.

The decisions we make today impact the life we build for ourselves tomorrow. Reading this book is one of those decisions. Just as there are multiple benefits to building a personal financial plan, there are benefits to taking a more proactive approach to building your own life plan. That's the power behind this book because if you have alignment and understanding, you have freedom. And that is the ultimate measure of any client-centric financial advisor—their ability to help you find your freedom.

Now is the time to think about your ideal, authentic life:

- What is it you value?
- What type of life will give you fulfillment and joy beyond measure?
- Who will you surround yourself with when sharing life together?

These are the questions I hope you ask yourself as you dive into chapter 1—and the truth I hope you accept for yourself after reading the approach Larry outlines in the chapters ahead.

Here's to finding your freedom, financially and beyond.

Ron Carson, Founder & CEO, Carson Group
Entrepreneur, Financial Advisor, Philanthropist,
New York Times Best-Selling Author,
Thought Leader

First, a Word About Joy

Joy: The emotion evoked by well-being, success, or good fortune or by the prospect of possessing what one desires: delight

A common theme you'll see throughout this book is *joy*. Many financial advisors and clients focus only on the monetary value of personal financial planning. At Mitlin Financial, we absolutely believe personal financial planning is essential to ensuring your and your family's financial well-being.

However, we view financial well-being as the means to the ultimate goal of experiencing joy in life, not as the goal itself.

We believe that the better you prepare and get your financial house in order, the more capacity you have to experience joy in your life. The more planning you do, the less worry you will likely experience about your future. That translates into more joy!

Life is hard. We all get bogged down with everyday responsibilities, challenges, and unexpected setbacks.

Often, the joy we naturally embraced as children sadly dissipates as we fight the battles of adulthood. So, as adults, we need to be intentional about finding the joy in life and making the most of it—just as we need to be intentional about preparing for a confident financial future.

In fact, we believe joy is so important to people's overall happiness, health, and well-being that we have trademarked this important question that we constantly ask ourselves and others:

What did you do today that brought you joy?®

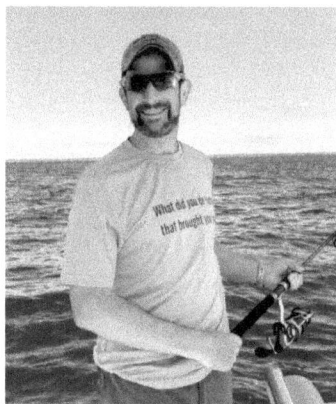

I have had this question printed on T-shirts, and I often wear these shirts when we go out to enjoy life. I love the responses from people! For example, one day, when I was wearing it, a woman came up to me and said, "Hershey's Kisses."

She had read my shirt and answered the question without even prefacing it by saying, "I saw your shirt." She just wanted to share that she had eaten some Hershey's chocolate Kisses that day, and it had brought her joy. What a great response! It shows that small things can bring us joy, maybe even more often than big things can.

At Mitlin Financial, we love bringing awareness to people about the importance of manifesting and embracing joy in life! I hope you learn, by reading this book, the importance of personal financial planning in optimizing the joy in your life.

Acknowledgments

Thank you to my wife, Denise, for your unwavering support in life and business and for helping me through the process of writing this book.

To our kids, Zachary and Jeremy, I appreciate that you are always supportive of everything I do. Thank you for coming up with great ideas that are helpful to the firm.

I want to thank and acknowledge Ron Carson, founder and CEO of the Carson Group, for your many years of partnership and for writing the excellent foreword for this book.

Many thanks to Mary Kate Gulick, CMO of the Carson Group, for your advice and guidance on the book's content, design, and release.

And to all the Mitlin Financial stakeholders and Carson Group stakeholders, I am grateful for the exceptional support, guidance, and help you provide in serving our families.

PART 1

Accumulating Your Retirement Savings

Preparing for retirement consists of two key phases—*accumulating* savings and *preserving* those savings. The two parts of this book address those phases, respectively.

Part 1 covers the following six chapters:

Discover Your *Why*

While serving families as a financial advisor for more than two decades, one comment I hear often is that people feel intimidated by the very thought of financial planning. There is an enduring but erroneous stigma that financial planning is complicated. This perception paralyzes many people to the point where it prevents them from engaging in the very process that could increase their financial confidence.

People are terrified that they will run out of money in retirement. Having this fear in the back of your mind at all times absolutely robs your life of confidence and joy. Having a personal financial plan developed by your fiduciary financial advisor is the best way to conquer that fear.

Concerns about being able to retire are reflected in the 2022 Schroders US Retirement Survey. It reveals that only 22 percent of people approaching retirement age believe they'll have enough money to maintain a comfortable standard of living. But the study also reveals an encouraging fact—building and maintaining a holistic financial plan has been proven to be an effective catalyst to a better financial outlook. According to the survey, 91 percent of those who have done retirement planning said it has been useful to them, and 33 percent reported it has been critical to putting them on a better path for retirement. Another survey from Charles Schwab found that people with written plans feel more confident and less stressed. Additional research reports that people with plans make better decisions, develop better financial habits, and have better financial outcomes.[1]

Building and maintaining a holistic financial plan has been proven to be an effective catalyst to a better financial outlook.

That research aligns with my experience in preparing personal financial plans for families during the past two decades.

I wrote this book because I want you to know that financial planning does not have to be complicated and that working with a *fiduciary* financial advisor to develop your personal financial plan can enhance your retirement experience significantly. A *fiduciary* is legally and morally obligated to act in your best interest *all the time*. In chapter 10, "The Value of a Fiduciary Advisor," I

---

1. "78% of People Aren't Ready for Retirement: The Good News? Everyone Can Improve Their Financial Prospects," Kathleen Coxwell, NewRetirement.com, May 26, 2022, https://www.newretirement.com/retirement/78-of-people-arent-ready-for-retirement-the-good-news-everyone-can-improve-their-financial-prospects/.

explain what that means, why it is incredibly important, and how to find a financial advisor who is a fiduciary. Partnering with a fiduciary advisor throughout your financial-planning journey will benefit you in every aspect of personal financial planning.

Like anything new you try—learning a new app, playing a new musical instrument, or driving in a place you've never visited—it's unfamiliar. Yet the rewards associated with pushing that fear aside to learn something new are tremendous. If you approach financial planning the right way, it can be a huge step for you toward living your best life. My hope is that this book will replace any intimidation you feel with knowledge and the inspiration to work with a competent fiduciary financial advisor to build your personal financial plan.

No two financial plans are alike. Your plan needs to be tailored to your unique situation, needs, goals, and vision. Financial planning is an investment in yourself, and the sooner you begin, the better. Investing in yourself when you are younger can afford you a better opportunity to achieve the life you desire.

Your Personal Financial Plan Is a "Hub"

Your personal financial plan is like the center of a wheel, the hub. The spokes of the wheel, which represent the different components of your plan, extend from the center and turn with the wheel. Everything is connected:

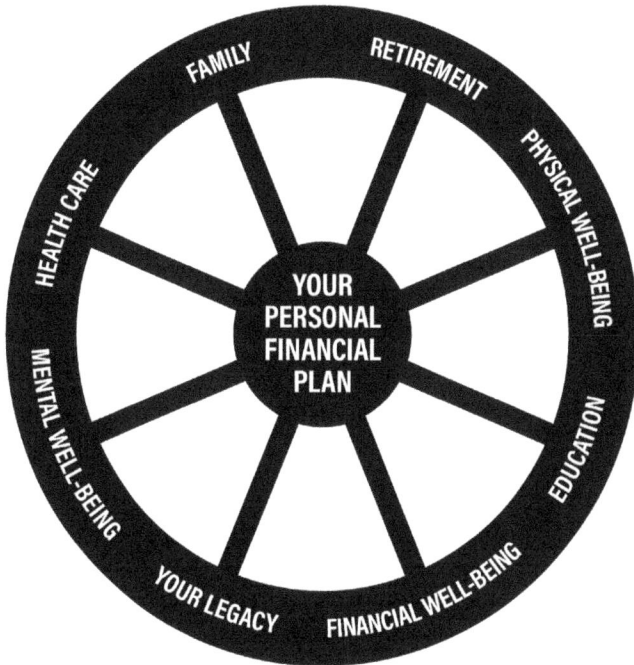

It's Not All About the Money—It's About Living Your Best Life

It's easy to see why financial planning intimidates many people—a lot of advisors and wealth-management firms focus on the dollars and cents. When they talk about retirement, they boil it down to "Here's how much you will need."

But personal financial planning is about much more than just the money.

Your financial well-being, both now and in retirement, is about living your best life possible. Because of the prevailing focus on the numbers, it often requires a mindset shift to begin thinking about retirement in terms of your quality of life, and joy, instead.

Retirement is a welcome event for many people. That's because they already know what types of activities they want to pursue that they never had time for while they were working. But retirement can be a major upheaval for many people, especially if their entire identities are tied up in their titles, careers, and professional accomplishments.

With proper planning, you can begin to slow down in your career gradually. Then, once you retire, you will already have some idea of how you will spend your extra time on activities that are personally meaningful to you.

I encourage you to start thinking about retirement in terms of your ideal life. Yes, the numbers are important, but money is only the means to the end. Once you know what you want your life to be like, then we can start proactively planning how you can go from where you are today to where you want to be, both financially and otherwise.

We see many people going through life focused on their daily routines, without really forming a vision of what they want out of life, now and in the future. This is the critical first step in personal financial planning—knowing why you are working so hard to earn money.

This is your "why," and it serves as the foundation for everything else.

Having a compelling *why* will inspire you to seek out a competent, compassionate, fiduciary financial advisor to work with and to follow the financial plan he or she develops with you. Discovering your *why* will give you clarity about what you are earning and saving money for and what you want to accomplish.

What Is Your "Why"?

Few parents teach their children the value of personal financial planning, mostly because they don't know about it themselves. Schools typically don't teach financial planning, either. This is why most people live their lives just moving from one life event to another as those events happen—not on the financial aspect of planning proactively for their best future.

They focus on their grades in school so they can get into a good college. In college, they focus on getting good grades so they will be competitive in the job market once they graduate. Once they begin their careers, they search for someone to spend their lives with. Then it's time to buy a home, start a family, and advance in their careers.

In my experience, once people slow down a little and become intentional about determining their "why," they get it. They see why it is the foundation for everything else to come. Life gets progressively more complicated, and you take on more responsibilities over time. Soon, you're so busy that you hardly have time to brush your teeth. That pace of life becomes the norm, and if you don't make personal planning a habit early on, it doesn't happen. Yet it's the most important step toward securing your best future!

When people get wrapped up in those natural life progressions, they typically don't spend the time, effort, and energy to sit down and find their "why." It requires a conscious effort to take this important step.

Your "Why" May Change Over Time

Some of your priorities in life—your "why"—will change over time. Others will stay the same, regardless of your age or life stage.

Everyone who knows my wife, Denise, and me knows that family is our biggest priority. Losing my mom to cancer at a young age affected me deeply. And then, after Denise and I were married about four years, Denise lost her brother at an early age to suicide. The families we serve know that family comes first for us—in fact, our devotion to family attracts many of the families Mitlin serves.

Having a strong "why," or sense of purpose, makes decisions easier. If you are faced with two conflicting priorities, you can simply choose the one that aligns more closely with your main priority. If I am expected to attend two different events on the same day at the same time, and one is for my family but the other one is not, I'm going to choose the family-related event.

Having a strong "why" gives you a compass for making decisions in life, both financial and otherwise. Knowing your "why" also gives you the power to say no to things that do not serve that "why."

If you are faced with two conflicting priorities, you can simply choose the one that aligns more closely with your main priority.

If you have a significant other, it is important to determine your *collective* "why"—your shared purpose and priorities. That will make it easier for you both to work toward your goals together. Of course you will both have goals that are personal to you and not shared, but striving toward some shared goals together can enrich your relationship.

In the next section, you will learn how a strong *why* led me to become a financial advisor.

Our Firm's Name Represents Our Family and Our Values

People often ask me, "Why is your firm called Mitlin Financial when your last name is Sprung?"

The answer to that question revolves around our family and the reason I am so passionate about guiding people to financial confidence.

An entrepreneurial spirit emerged in me when I was just a kid. Starting at age eleven, I had a paper route. That was before electronic payments came along, so newspaper carriers had to go door-to-door to collect payments. Yep, that was me, every day, walking or riding my bike to my neighbors' homes. I really enjoyed interacting with people and learning more about them.

We were neither poor nor wealthy; we were a middle-class family. My dad was a New York City schoolteacher, and he had his own business on the side as well—what we now call a side hustle (more about that in chapter 3).

My mom, Linda, was diagnosed with breast cancer when I was just a kid. She was young—in her thirties. I watched her battle the disease for more than a decade. We ended up losing her when she was only forty-seven.

When she was ill, my dad did a great job taking care of her, as well as my sister and me. I remember watching him struggle with all his responsibilities— taking care of all of us, running our household, managing her care and the bills associated with it, working as a teacher, and running his side business. He did not have a financial advisor.

As I got older and headed to college, I became aware of the value of professional financial advice. I often thought that if my dad had worked with a financial advisor, it could have mitigated some of the difficulties he experienced. It wouldn't have changed my mom's health situation or the fact that he was juggling a lot of responsibilities, but it probably would have helped him manage it all better. He would have had somebody he could call to discuss roadblocks or hurdles he was encountering. And he probably could have relaxed and enjoyed life more.

That reality resonated and stuck with me. It's one of the main reasons I decided to become a financial advisor. I felt it would be very rewarding to be in a career that enabled me to design financial road maps to help guide people's future. I had a strong desire to help families navigate the challenges they faced in their lives that affected both their finances and their quality of life, such as a serious illness. I also wanted to guide families as they navigated happy events, such as planning for a wedding, buying a home, or sending a child off to college.

In high school, my friends and I watched CNBC and paid attention to stocks and the market. (Not typical for most high-schoolers, I know.). So, by the time I got to Binghamton University in south central New York, I was somewhat aware of the value financial advisors provide to their clients.

One of my college housemates had an internship with Dean Witter. At one time, Dean Witter Reynolds was one of the largest firms in the securities industry and was among the largest members of the New York Stock Exchange. (I am dating myself a bit here because after several mergers, that company no longer exists.)

That housemate approached me and our other housemates one day and said, "Hey, my internship is coming to an end. The person who runs the office is looking for somebody to take over my role. Is anybody interested?"

I said, "Yes, I'm interested." I stepped into his role and watched how advisors worked with clients.

It gave me a great opportunity to experience what the career would be like. I saw that, as an advisor, I could set my own hours, to some extent. More importantly, it was fulfilling for me to see advisors serving families and helping them set and reach goals. I knew it was a career I could do for a very long time and that I would always feel good about the work I was doing.

A few months after my mom passed away, I began dating Denise, who is now my wife. Before Denise and I met, she had been living in Philadelphia, Pennsylvania, and I was living in Rockland County, New York. By the time we met, though, she had moved back to Long Island. I asked her, "What brought you back from Philly?" She said her grandfather had been terminally ill, and she wanted to spend time with him and the rest of her family.

During that conversation, we learned that my mom, Linda, and Denise's grandfather, Mitchell, had passed away within several hours of each other, a few months prior to us meeting online.

When I launched my own financial services firm in 2004, I wanted to choose a name that really meant something and that would continue to impact people's lives even after I'm gone. So I combined the "Mit" in Denise's grandfather's name, Mitchell, with the "Lin" in my mom's name, Linda, to form the name "Mitlin."

Naming the firm after these two strong people of character is fitting. Denise and I did so not only because we wanted to memorialize them, but also because they both possessed characteristics we want to reflect in the way we do business.

My mom was a fighter, a warrior—one of the most courageous people I've ever known. She taught me the importance of family, being level-headed, and maintaining a courageous attitude. She battled cancer for thirteen years, tooth and nail, and she did it with a smile all along the way. She used to say, "Everything's meant to be," and she actually meant it. She was a great human being and role model.

Mitchell was a hard-working man of character who was devoted to his family. A World War II veteran and New York City police officer, he was known for being a good listener and a generous soul. He was the Grandpa who bought everyone on the block ice cream when the ice cream truck came—he wasn't wealthy, but it warmed his heart to see all those smiling faces.

So Denise and I felt that naming the firm after my mom and her grandpa would be a meaningful way to honor these two special people and to create a firm that represents those same values. In many regards, the families we serve at Mitlin Financial represent those same values, which has created a family-like environment. The people who work in our firm and the people we serve are family to us.

"Is There a Fit?"

We are very protective of the values we abide by and the family environment we've created here, through and through—the company, our stakeholders, and the families we serve. For this reason, not everybody becomes a client of Mitlin Financial. We are selective in who we work with. To determine which families we will work with, we use what we call the "Is there a fit?" process.

In fact, we call our first meeting with a potential client the "Is there a fit?" meeting. We have a fifteen- or twenty-minute conversation with the family. We discuss their goals and objectives in working with us and what they're looking for in an advisor. Then we outline what we're looking for in the families we serve. We ask the family to think about whether or not they think we're a good fit for them, and at the same time, my team and I evaluate whether we think the family is a good fit for us.

If it seems to be a good fit on both sides, we then will move forward and schedule the next meeting. If it's not a good fit, we will help them as best we can, maybe by referring them to another firm or advisor who might be a better fit. Sometimes, though, we'll just part and go our separate ways.

It is extremely important for us to lead the families we work with in creating intergenerational wealth. We believe we can make the biggest impact on families when they understand the value of long-term planning to help secure future generations. Today, we are working with the second and third generations of our original client families. We're not looking for client relationships that last six months or one or two years. We want to become an extension of the families we serve and guide them in protecting their financial assets from one generation to the next.

> **It is extremely important for us to lead the families we work with in creating intergenerational wealth.**

We also enjoy working with high earners who are not rich yet. These are people who have a long runway before retirement and can benefit most from long-term planning. People who have a short runway before retiring will not be able to reap the benefits of long-term planning. This was the case with a gentleman who called me one Wednesday a few years ago.

He called in cold and asked for me. When I got to the phone, he said, "I need some help. I'm retiring from my company, and I want to know if I have enough money and assets to be able to retire."

I said, "OK, then let's set up a meeting. I'm booked the rest of this week. Would you be able to meet next Tuesday or Wednesday to discuss this and see how we might be able to help you?"

"Oh no, no. I can't wait that long," he replied. "I'm retiring on Friday."

"Friday—two days from now?"

He said yes. I asked him how I would be able to help him.

"We could go over some numbers," he suggested.

"That's not the service we provide," I told him. "Typically, we're working with people at least a year, and preferably five or ten years, before they retire. I cannot help you much by meeting with you on Thursday when you're retiring on Friday."

This gentlemen simply had no runway left in his career to benefit from the service we provide and the tools we offer for long-term planning. As much as I wished I could have helped this gentleman a few years earlier, he just wasn't a fit for our firm when he came to us.

The Earlier You Begin Planning, the Better

From a financial-planning perspective, the more time you have before retirement when you begin planning, the better.

The primary benefit of beginning to save early is that you can grow your money over time, thanks to compound interest. Albert Einstein said, "Compound interest is the eighth wonder of the world. He who understands it earns it; he who doesn't pays it."

According to a study from Vanguard, if you began saving $10,000 per year at age 25 and continued until you were 45 years old, you could have more than $1 million by the time you reached retirement age. However, if you waited until you were 35 to begin saving, and you contributed the same $10,000 per year to your savings until you were 65, you would retire with less than $840,000.[2]

A second benefit of having a personal financial plan prepared for you early is that your advisor can adjust your financial plan as needed when your circumstances change. Sometimes, even minor adjustments will lead to major improvements in your financial situation. All of us constantly face changes in our situations, as well as changes in the markets and economy.

If you're only three to five years from retirement, you can still benefit from developing a personal financial plan. However, you will have fewer tools to aid you in making adjustments.

---

2. "When Should You Start Saving for Retirement? Vanguard, date unknown, https://investor.vanguard.com/investor-resources-education/retirement/savings-when-to-start.

Write Down Your Goals

Setting goals is a big part of planning, whether you are remodeling your kitchen, planning a vacation, or building a financial plan. Once you know what you're striving for, then we build your personal financial plan, which will guide you in every decision you make. Having a plan will provide guidelines for keeping you on track as you pursue your goals. This might mean setting a budget and sticking to it, which we discuss in chapter 3.

We are much more likely to reach our goals if we write them down. Part of the reason this is true lies in the way our brains work.

Having a plan will provide guidelines for keeping you on track as you pursue your goals.

Research shows that writing down your goals improves the brain's encoding process. *Encoding* is the biological process by which the things we perceive travel to the brain's hippocampus, where they're analyzed. From there, we make decisions about what gets stored in our long-term memory and what gets discarded. When you write down something such as a goal, there is a much greater chance that you will remember it. Plus, neuropsychologists say that individuals demonstrate better memory for material they have generated themselves than for material they've merely read.[3]

In my work with families, I have seen that those who take the time to identify their "why," write it down, and specify goals that will lead them to achieve their best lives possible tend to enjoy better outcomes. After you write down your goals, keep them in a place—or several places—where you will see them often. Writing them down causes you to consciously commit to achieving them. Keeping your goals and your "why" visible, so you can read them often, will drive you and inspire you to focus on activities that will move you closer toward your best life.

Taking the time to envision your ideal life, discover your "why," and write down goals to help you achieve that life creates space for your life to be more meaningful. This will lead you to focus on both qualitative and quantitative goals that are really important to you.

Prior Planning Can Prevent Panic

A while back, a potential client and his wife contacted our firm, and we met with them. After our preliminary discussion, we wanted to gather their

---

3. "Neuroscience Explains Why You Need to Write Down Your Goals if You Actually Want to Achieve Them," Mark Murphy, *Forbes*, April 15, 2018, https://www.forbes.com/sites/markmurphy/2018/04/15/neuroscience-explains-why-you-need-to-write-down-your-goals-if-you-actually-want-to-achieve-them/.

information and begin putting a personal financial plan together. But they were not ready, for whatever reason.

Two years later, the husband called me, frantic because he learned that the company that had employed him for many years might be closing. He told me, "Hey, I need to know that if they close, am I going to be in a position that I can retire or slow down?"

I said, "I really can't give you that assessment without sitting down and getting all that information we had talked about getting originally and putting a financial plan together for you."

"Well, you can't just give me an idea?"

"You are asking me to give you a diagnosis about your financial health without having seen you for two years and knowing nothing about your current situation," I replied. "In the medical world, that would be malpractice."

I encouraged him to come to our office, sit down with us, provide us with vital information, and move forward with the financial plan. We did that, and luckily for him, we discovered that as long as he worked at some kind of part-time job, which he was willing to do, he would be successful in retiring if the company closed down.

His company didn't shut down, though. This man ended up retiring on his own from the company about six years after that, so it was a nonevent. But during that time when he was in panic mode, it was an emergency situation for him. He needed answers. Had he engaged us earlier, and we started the planning like we wanted to, we could have easily assured him that his financial situation was such that he would be OK financially if his company shut down—as long as he worked part-time somewhere.

Without having a plan in place, it's not easy for us to make that type of assessment about a given "What if?" scenario.

Many people view a financial plan as a static document they have to follow—or that they look at once and put away. It's not. A personal financial plan is a dynamic road map that guides you from where you are now to where you want to be. It makes it easier to adjust your plan when you face unexpected life events, whether they're positive or negative. Your personal plan is a valuable tool that allows us to evaluate how a life event, whether positive or negative, is going to impact your overall situation.

Not only is your financial plan a valuable guide for making decisions and planning how to navigate changes in your life; it also provides you with a level of financial confidence that you likely cannot attain without it. When you have your personal plan in place, you will be less likely to panic when something in your life or in the economy shifts. You can simply meet with your advisor to reevaluate your situation and see how it looks financially, rather than having to start from ground zero.

Combining Effective Asset Management with a Personal Financial Plan

Many times, people come to us because they're not sure how well they are positioning themselves for retirement. Unfortunately, this can be the case even when they are already working with a financial advisor.

As opposed to calling this type of review a "second opinion," we prefer to discuss how, sometimes, *minor adjustments can lead to major improvements.*

One day, a woman reached out and asked us for an appointment, and we scheduled an "Is there a fit?" call. She told us the name of the advisor she was working with. I happen to know the name, and I typed it into the FINRA BrokerCheck[4] website, which anybody can use to check out the background of an advisor in our profession. She was not aware that many complaints had been issued against him over the previous several years.

When she came into our office, we reviewed her statements and gathered more information from her. As

4. The Financial Industry Regulatory Authority (FINRA) is a private, American, self-regulatory corporation that regulates member brokerage firms and exchange markets. FINRA BrokerCheck tells you instantly whether a person or firm is registered, as required by law, to sell securities (stocks, bonds, mutual funds, and more), offer investment advice, or both. On the site, you also can browse the list of brokers barred by FINRA and see any formal actions the SEC has brought against individuals, including those who are not brokers. Go to https://brokercheck.finra.org/.

we reviewed her accounts, a couple of things came to light very quickly.

First, the accounts were not really in line with her appropriate asset allocation. And second, we discovered that she was paying a commission on every single transaction. In 2021 alone, there had been about 110 transactions in a single account. It was a commission-based account, so she was paying the advisor a commission on every trade. That one account cost her almost 3 percent of the value of her portfolio, which is much more than I believe she should have been paying. She was paying the advisor on a per-trade or transaction basis, rather than paying an asset-based fee or a fee for service. This means the advisor was receiving an incentive to trade the account. He made money when he traded the account.

Not only that—the advisor had not worked with her to develop a financial plan. Although she was paying a sizable sum of money, she had no formal plan in place to prepare for retirement. That alone had made her question whether she was receiving an appropriate level of service.

Now that she is working with us, we are managing her accounts on her behalf in a manner that aligns with her risk tolerance, goal, and objectives. We are also developing a personal financial plan that will guide her to and through retirement. Using that plan as the starting point, it will be easy for us to show her where she is now, where she's going, and how she can make progress toward those goals. She has thanked us on numerous occasions already and is really enjoying being part of the Mitlin family.

This scenario happens more often that it should. Again, I strongly advise you to seek out a financial advisor who is a "fiduciary"—one who is obligated to act in clients' best interests. Not all financial advisors are fiduciaries. We discuss this topic more in chapter 10.

Practicing What I Teach

It's hard to imagine how this could be possible, but there are insurance agents and financial advisors out there who stress to their clients the importance of protecting their families' futures with planning, yet they do not do it for themselves. Since before entering this profession, I understood the importance of practicing what we teach. If we aim to be positive role models for the families we serve, we need to follow our own advice.

This is so important to me, in fact, that I established a 529 plan—a college savings plan—for my children, years before I had children! I named myself as the beneficiary, and when our children were born, I named them as the beneficiaries. That planning put Denise and me in the significant position that we are now paying for our children's college education with money we saved over the years. Because we began planning so early, approximately 70 cents on every dollar that we are pulling out of our older son's college savings plan is growth, and only 30 cents on every dollar is money that we put into the plan.

This is just one example of the tremendous value you can derive by beginning to plan early.

Now that you realize the importance of having a compelling "why," we will discuss, in chapter 2, a valuable strategy you can follow. It's a three-word mantra that many successful people follow to make the most of their financial situations: "Pay yourself first."

Chapter 1—Making It Personal

1. What is your "why"—in other words, why are you working so hard? What do you hope to accomplish? What does your ideal life look like, now and once you retire? What are your current priorities?
2. How many years do you plan to continue working before you retire? What do you want your life to look like before you retire? After you retire? Write down specific aspects of what your ideal life looks like for both time frames—not

just financially, but personally as well.

3. Once you retire, what are you going to do with your extra time? What types of activities do you want to pursue that are personally meaningful to you? How will your priorities change when you're no longer working? How will your daily routine change? How might your relationships change?

4. To what extent could you ease into retirement gradually instead of going straight from working full-time to not working at all? How might a gradual transition make retirement easier for you?

5. What did you do today that brought you joy?*

Pay Yourself First

Proof that financial planning is not complicated lies in the brief but powerful mantra "Pay yourself first." Following this one simple strategy can improve your financial well-being.

My first introduction to this compelling truth was when I read the book *The Richest Man in Babylon*, a classic book that George S. Clason published in 1926. In it, Clason shares parables by a fictional Babylonian character named Arkad, a poor scribe who became the "richest man in Babylon." Arkad then offers advice for others to follow, including the "Seven Cures" (how to generate wealth) and the "Five Laws of Gold" (how to protect and invest wealth).

That book hammered home to me the importance of paying yourself a percentage of your earnings before you pay your debts. Reading the book made me realize that Clason's approach is the opposite approach that most people take. When most people get paid, they pay everyone else what they owe—the rent or mortgage, utilities, food, and bills—and then figure out how to manage the amount that's left.

I agree with Clason that we have been doing this backwards. We need to pay ourselves first to honor that compelling *why* we discussed in chapter 1. We are not working hard to pay the mortgage and bills; we are working to be fundamentally financially sound and to achieve the goals we've set for living our best lives.

Why do we feel compelled to pay everyone but ourselves first? I don't know the answer to that, but because it is so ingrained in us, it requires a conscious mindset shift to turn it around. We need to deem ourselves the most important part of the equation instead of the least important.

> **We need to pay ourselves first to honor that compelling *why* we discussed in chapter 1.**

Decide How Much to Pay Yourself

When we meet with families, we talk about this concept and encourage them to follow this valuable advice.

A good percentage to start out with is 10 percent—when you get paid, put aside 10 percent of that money in an account for yourself, and then pay your bills. Allocate that money to your emergency fund, your retirement plan, and other "buckets" of money that will benefit you personally.

If you are unable to begin with 10 percent, start

with whatever number works for you, whether it's 5 or 6 percent or some other number. Then, as you're able, tick that amount up over the next several months. For example, you could set aside 5 percent of your income for a couple of months and then dial it up to 6 percent, and then 7 percent, until you get to 10 percent or beyond.

If your income is $10,000 per month and you're earning $3,000 per month from a side hustle, then your income is $13,000 per month, and we recommend putting away 10 percent of that—$1,300—before you pay anyone else. Paying yourself that first 10 percent of your income will ensure that at least that amount of your income will benefit you at some point in the future.

Some of the families we work with began using this concept with their employer-sponsored 401(k) plans. When they began participating in the plan, they were contributing 3 percent of their income. Now, with the "Pay yourself first" concept in mind, we encourage them to bump that up to 4 percent to see what the impact is. They typically discover that putting an extra 1 percent into their retirement account doesn't affect their income as much as they expected—especially because the money they're setting aside is pre-tax dollars. One dollar they put into their 401(k) account actually represents less than one dollar of their paycheck because they are taxed less on that money than on the money they do not contribute to the 401(k).

We encourage them to contribute 4 percent and then 5 percent and upward, until they get to a point where they do start to feel their income being affected— to their borderline comfort level. In many cases, we've seen people increase their automatic deferrals to 10 or 15 percent as a result of this strategy.

This growth in retirement savings is enhanced further when there is an employer match, which is common. It is important to find out if your employer has a match on its retirement plan and what percentage of your income you must contribute to receive that match. You want to put in at least that amount; otherwise, you are leaving money on the table. Again, the sooner you begin putting money away into a retirement account, the more time that money has to grow, thanks to the power of compound interest.

Here is an example[5] that shows just how big a difference saving money can benefit you, especially if you start early. As shown in the chart below, our hypothetical client, Pat, saved money in an interest-bearing account from the ages of 20 through 45 and then stopped. Kelly didn't start saving money in a similar account until age 45 and continued saving until age 65. Because of the powerful effect of compound

---

5. "The Magic of Compounding & How I Should be Retired by Now," Robert Roy Britt, Medium.com, February 25, 2019, https://robertroybritt.medium.com/the-magic-of-compounding-how-i-couldve-been-retired-by-now-c30a5e21200a.

interest, Pat ended up with a retirement account worth $2,039,104, while Kelly's was worth only $895,444. Yet Pat invested only $91,000, compared to Kelly's investment of $336,000.

How Investing Early Impacts Retirement Income

Age	Pat		Kelly	
	Amount Invested	Year-End Value	Amount Invested	Year-End Value
19	$0	$0		
20	$1,000	$1,100		
21	$1,200	$2,530		
22	$1,400	$4,323		
23	$1,600	$6,515		
24	$1,800	$9,147		
25	$2,000	$12,262		
26	$2,200	$15,908		
27	$2,400	$20,138		
28	$2,600	$25,012		
29	$2,800	$30,594		
30	$3,000	$36,593		
31	$3,200	$44,168		
32	$3,400	$52,325		
33	$3,600	$61,517		
34	$3,800	$71,849		
35	$4,000	$83,434		
36	$4,200	$96,398		
37	$4,400	$110,877		
38	$4,600	$127,025		
39	$4,800	$145,007		

Age	Pat Amount Invested	Pat Year-End Value	Kelly Amount Invested	Kelly Year-End Value
40	$5,000	$165,008		
41	$5,200	$187,229		
42	$5,400	$211,892		
43	$5,600	$239,241		
44	$5,800	$269,545		
45	$6,000	$303,100	$6,000	$6,600
46		$333,410	$7,000	$14,960
47		$366,751	$8,000	$25,256
48		$403,426	$9,000	$37,682
49		$443,768	$10,000	$52,450
50		$488,145	$11,000	$69,795
51		$536,960	$12,000	$89,974
52		$590,656	$13,000	$113,272
53		$649,721	$14,000	$139,999
54		$714,694	$15,000	$170,499
55		$786,163	$16,000	$105,149
56		$884,779	$17,000	$244,363
57		$951,257	$18,000	$288,600
58		$1,046,383	$19,000	$338,360
59		$1,151,021	$20,000	$394,196
60		$1,266,1233	$21,000	$456,715
61		$1,392,736	$22,000	$526,587
62		$1,532,009	$23,000	$604,545
63		$1,685,210	$24,000	$691,400
64		$1,853,731	$25,000	$788,040
65		**$2,039,104**	$26,000	**$895,444**
Total Invested		$91,000		$336,000
Net Earnings		**$1,948,104**		**$559,444**
Growth		2,041%		67%

The figures in this hypothetical example assume a 10 percent annual return.

Where Does Your Money Go?

Almost always, when people put their spending under a microscope to find out where their money is going, they are surprised to find that they are spending money on things they don't really want or need. It can feel intimidating to do this exercise, but it is a necessary step toward building your personal financial plan.

Examining your spending will enable you to be more mindful about whether or not you are spending your money toward the priorities and goals you have established. When you discover unnecessary spending, deploy that money toward better uses. This one exercise often brings to light at least 10 percent of people's income that they can use to pay themselves first.

Set Up Different Accounts for Different Purposes

Many people have just a checking account and a savings account. I believe we can do a better job of allocating money toward various priorities if we set up accounts dedicated to those various priorities.

The tendency is to funnel all income into one account and then pay all the bills out of that account. Again, with the traditional mindset, whatever is left over is ours, and then we might move some of that money into savings. If an emergency comes up, we pay for it out of the same checking account. In that scenario, it's difficult to see what money is going where.

Setting up several different accounts makes it easier to segregate your money as soon as you earn it. For example, consider setting up a checking account that is your emergency fund—money that's dedicated to the inevitable unexpected expenses that crop up. That could be a vehicle repair, a home repair, a medical emergency, or something else. Promise yourself you will access that money only in an emergency. (Sorry, but deciding to take a weekend trip to the beach or mountains doesn't constitute an emergency!)

> **I believe we can do a better job of allocating money toward various priorities if we set up accounts dedicated to those various priorities.**

If one of the priorities you have identified is going on a big vacation, saving for a child's upcoming wedding, or buying a lake house, set up a savings account specifically for that, and contribute a percentage of your income to it each month. Whatever your priorities are, define a game plan for the amount of money you're putting into each account on a regular basis. Your financial advisor will help you establish this game plan as a part of designing your personal financial plan.

As soon as you receive any type of income, dole that money out to your various accounts. The only money that should be left in your checking account is money you need to pay your regular monthly bills.

Having separate accounts gives you more clarity about what your priorities are and where your money is going. It makes it easier for you to put money aside and separate specific expenses from your regular day-to-day cash flow. Again, much of this is a mindset issue. If all your money is in one checking account, it's easy to lose track of it and spend it on everything but your top priorities. You feel like all that money is there and available for whatever you need.

But if you've set aside money in specific accounts, it reminds you of your various priorities and makes it easier to honor them. You are mentally preparing yourself that if you have extra money in your checking account, that money is not to be used for emergencies or a vacation.

An Emergency Fund Will Minimize Disruptions to Your Lifestyle

An emergency fund is a must for protecting your lifestyle in the event of a disaster, whether it's an economic downturn, loss of property due to a fire or flood, the premature death of a loved one, or something else.

Depending on your personal circumstances, we recommend having three to eighteen months' worth of income set aside for emergencies. If your income is regular and predictable, such as a paycheck from an employer, then one year's worth of income might be sufficient. But for people whose income is somewhat erratic, such as the self-employed, we advise a more conservative amount, on the eighteen-month side. We have had self-employed clients who made $20,000 from a consulting agreement one month but had little or no income the next month. A game plan is critically important in this type of situation.

Having this money set aside will make a significant difference in your ability to pay yourself and your bills in the event that hard times come around.

Corporate executives who lose their jobs or decide to pursue other opportunities might need only three to six months' worth of savings if they are able to land new positions quickly. Again, your financial advisor will work with you to determine an appropriate amount for you to save in an emergency fund. The amount will depend on several factors, including how much money you have saved for retirement, how much debt you have, and what your financial and lifestyle goals are.

Once you have built your emergency fund up to that appropriate level, then you will no longer need to contribute money to that account because you are saving your income in various accounts. As soon as you spend that money on an emergency, build it back up for the next one.

On the flip side, if you have no emergency fund, but you have a lot of money in your retirement plan, you might want to direct more of that 10 percent to your emergency fund to start building it up.

As you can see, every component of your financial plan is personal—there's no solution that will be right for everybody. In our experience, the people who use a systematic approach to taking care of themselves first end up in a far better financial position than those who don't.

Why Few People Follow This Wise Approach

Like many things in life, I think a lot of people inherently understand this concept and agree that it makes sense, but they don't actually follow it, for whatever reason.

In some cases, it's because of a lack of education— people don't know about this simple but powerful concept. Others are aware of the concept but fail to follow it because they have no one to help keep them accountable. That is another valuable benefit of working with a fiduciary financial advisor—he or she serves an important role of being an accountability partner to guide you in reaching your goals.

Still others ignore this concept because they have never taken the time to determine their *why*. They don't know what they're working toward, so they don't focus on specific priorities.

Credit Card Debt Is Evil!

I believe there is never a good reason to carry credit card debt. It is evil because it diminishes your financial well-being and erodes your progress toward your long-term financial goals.

It's not that I don't believe in using credit cards; I use them virtually exclusively. Credit cards come with some nice benefits, such as points toward travel, extended warranties, fraud protection, and cash back. However, I pay off the cards in full every month so I don't pay the typically high interest rates they charge. They are great tools if you use them properly. My advice is to charge a purchase to a credit card only if you know you can pay it off in full when the bill comes due.

I believe there is never a good reason to carry credit card debt.

If you already have credit card debt, work with your financial advisor on a game plan to pay all of it off. There are several approaches, and the one that is right for you depends on your overall situation. In this case, it is important to strike a balance between paying yourself first and paying off your debt.

The interest people pay on credit cards is often equal to the percentage they have committed to paying themselves first. Extinguish any credit card debt as soon as possible! The first step toward doing that is to stop using your cards. Get out of the habit. If you continue to run up credit card debt, it will be problematic to you and your ability to reach your financial goals. This is true even if you owe a small amount. Interest rates in the double digits add up quickly.

Pursue What Brings You Joy

In chapter 1, I stressed that having a strong *why*—a strong purpose for working—will guide the decisions you make. Similarly, identifying whatever brings you joy will inspire you to be disciplined about paying yourself first.

Again, this is different for everyone. Some people enjoy going out to dinner in fine restaurants. Others enjoy hobbies like golfing, boating, or traveling. When you adopt this "pay myself first" mentality, it makes you more mindful of the fact that you are deliberately paying yourself first so you can enjoy the things that bring you joy.

Most people don't have a clear idea of what they're spending their money on.

Most people don't have a clear idea of what they're spending their money on. And many don't realize that they are spending more than they are making. When we see that happening, we have to bring it to the attention of the families we serve. We tell them they are cash-flow-negative and that they need to figure out a solution for how to eliminate a certain amount of money from their current expenditures if they want to reach the goals they have set.

If you already have an ample emergency fund and an ample retirement fund, it is still important to pay yourself that first 10 percent (or whatever percent you decide on) first. We just emerged from a long period of unprecedented low interest rates. At that time, I would not have recommended putting your 10 percent into a bank account because you would have earned close to zero on it. Instead, I would recommend putting that money into a 529 plan for your children's college education or some other account.

As you continue to pay yourself first, continue to evaluate where to deposit that first 10 percent of your income. Make sure your money contributes to the areas of your financial situation that will benefit you the most in the long term. There is a certain level of responsibility for each of us to make sure the money we pay to ourselves first is being put to good use.

There is no question that there is significant value in working with a competent, experienced, compassionate fiduciary financial advisor. He or she will brainstorm with you, build your personal financial plan based on your unique situation and dreams, and serve as your accountability partner.

Chapter 2—Making It Personal

1. If you have not yet begun to pay yourself first, commit to doing so. What percentage of your income will you set aside for yourself, before you pay your bills? Try to begin with 10 percent.

2. If you have a 401(k) plan through your employer, increase the amount of your current contribution by at least 1 percent. If your employer provides a matching contribution, make sure you are meeting that minimum contribution so you can receive the match.

3. Analyze the past two or three months of expenditures in your checking account. Which expenditures do not align with your top priorities for your best life? Eliminate them, and use that money to pay yourself first.

4. If you do not currently have several bank accounts for separate expenses, set them up. Decide which accounts you will need, such as an emergency account, a vacation account, and a special-event account.

5. What did you do today that brought you joy?®

"Budget" Isn't a Dirty Word

In chapter 1, I mentioned that the very thought of financial planning scares a lot of people. The thought of setting up a budget—and following it—might be even more terrifying for many people.

It doesn't need to be. A budget is a simple yet powerful mindfulness tool that keeps you on track with your goals. The simple exercise of discovering what money comes in and goes out every month is a necessary starting point for following your personal financial plan.

When we begin to work with people to develop their personal financial plans, we try our darndest to get them involved in the budgeting process, even if it's just making a list of their overall expenses and income. We just need an idea of how much they are spending so we can calculate future income needs. For people who are planning for retirement, the two biggest factors that will impact their future are the amount of money they will need on an annual basis and how long that money will have to last.

Yet budgeting is one of the most difficult exercises for people to do. I think it is because most people don't have a good handle on their budgets—or they don't want to know!

Here's just one of many examples I could cite about people not wanting to admit how much they're spending.

Recently, while managing assets for a couple we work with, we gave them the budget worksheet we use and asked them to fill it out so we could get an idea of how much they spend on a monthly basis. We needed that information to project what their income needs might be in retirement. They did not get this information back to us in a timely fashion, despite some prompting. The husband finally replied to us in an email, "I got hung up on the budget because as I looked at the numbers, I realized I've been spending too much recently. I just don't want to look at the numbers!"

Yes, it can be uncomfortable—scary, even—to discover how much money you spend each month. It can be even more uncomfortable for a third party, such as your financial advisor, to know this information. This is a key reason many people shy away from budgeting. But it is a necessary step in making your money work harder for your future.

In a given year, as a family, you may look to reduce your dining out to experience a more luxurious family vacation. Another year, or years, you may look to reduce the money you are spending on vacations to increase your retirement or education funding. Budgeting comes down to the money available to your household and the priorities you have in mind for those funds. This can and will most likely shift and change over time.

The important thing when crafting a budget is understanding what money is coming in each month and where that money is going. Having a thoughtful process that documents your spending will allow you to review whether you are on or off budget and evaluate areas where you could reduce or increase spending or saving to meet your goals.

Sometimes, cutting back on expenses is easy. We have found that when people begin tracking the amount of money they spend on various categories, they realize that they are spending money on things they no longer use, such as subscriptions to online services or magazines. You can make a noticeable dent in your spending simply by eliminating a few expenses you don't need or want.

Sometimes, cutting back on expenses is easy.

You may also find success calling providers and negotiating down your monthly bills. I have personally had success doing this. Recently, my wife called the alarm company that services our home and the Mitlin offices, and after she negotiated with them, we were able to save hundreds of dollars yearly. Taking the time once a year to contact providers you pay monthly can add up to real savings.

There is a limited number of factors, or levers, you can change when planning for the future. You can change how much you earn, how much you spend, how much you are saving, your time horizon until retirement, and your risk profile. This is why it is critical to know how much money you are spending. If there is a gap between your spending and your income and future goals, then you must change one of those factors.

Awareness is the first step to seeing where you stand and planning for the future so you can get where you want to be.

Why Budgets Have Gotten a Bad Reputation

One reason people think of "budget" or "budgeting" as a dirty word is because the process is often associated with "spend shaming." Well-meaning parents, grandparents, mentors, and even financial advisors who are trying to encourage people to rein in their spending end up, instead, making them feel guilty about spending their money on the things that bring them joy.

So, in many people's minds, "budget" has become synonymous with the concept of limitations and restrictions.

This is why many people tend to resist the idea of working with a financial advisor on budgeting. They assume the advisor is going to tell them they can't go on vacation, eat at restaurants, or buy a newer car. Some advisors do take that approach, unfortunately.

We realize that the way people spend money is extremely personal. When we look at someone else's budget, we might think a certain expense is frivolous, but that might be something that brings the person a lot of joy. For this reason, we take the position at Mitlin Financial that we do not do budgeting for the families we serve. We want to use the budget as a tool to get an idea of their current spending so we can determine their income needs in the future. Yet we leave the budgeting details to each individual, couple, or family because again, it is extremely personal.

Whatever brings you joy should be a priority for you. And yes, following a budget will make it easier for you to reach your financial goals faster and stay on track—but the purpose of a budget isn't to eliminate the things you enjoy. The purpose is to determine if there is a gap between people's monthly spending and the amount of money they bring in. If there is a gap, we let them know how much it is and recommend that they work with their spouse and family to cut back their spending by at least that amount. The idea is to make sure we have accurate numbers as we build their personal financial plan and that it will keep them on track for a

Whatever brings you joy should be a priority for you.

long period of time.

The key is to be mindful about what you want to accomplish in your life, what you want to experience and enjoy, and how you are spending your money as you set out to achieve those goals. We all have different interests and priorities in life, and I believe it is never appropriate to approach budgeting from a judgmental standpoint.

Moderation is an art form that is beneficial to most of us. We just want you to balance the joy of experiences you have now with the financial confidence you have about having a comfortable retirement. You don't have to choose between having fun now or living well later; the idea is to balance the two.

For example, let's say you have a rather expensive gym membership that offers services like therapeutic massage, personal training, and nutrition counseling. Those services are probably beneficial, or necessary, for your physical and mental health, and they bring you joy. It is no one else's place to cast judgment on you about that expense and "spend-shame" you. Instead, that membership is a key expense—an important part of your lifestyle—that needs to be at the top of your list of priorities.

Personally, I enjoy Starbucks, and I will continue going there as long as I can afford it. But if a time came when I could not afford it, or I needed to sacrifice that indulgence for another necessary expense, I would have to look at it realistically. If I had two competing expenses in my budget, and I needed to cut one, I would cut the one that brings me less joy than the other. But before I can do that, I have to identify what brings me the most joy in life.

A Budget Doesn't Have to Be Restrictive

Composing and following a budget does not have to be restrictive. It is vital to have a thoughtful process outlining what your needs and wants are and the dollars and cents associated with each.

Needs are things that are must-haves for you and your family, such as food, shelter, and clothing. Depending on your situation, travel or gym memberships may be needed to maintain your family's mental or physical health. Your *wants* list should include things you would like to add to the budget if there is sufficient money available for you to have or enjoy, above your savings and needs.

A budget will help you prioritize the expenses that should be part of your budget, create the budget, and track it over time. Yes, you might end up having to cut back in some areas, depending on what your situation looks like. But without a budget, you'll never know.

If you have enough after-tax income to cover all your fixed and variable expenses, and you are comfortable with that level of spending, then you can probably keep it that way and still reach your goals. There's no reason to make any adjustments. However, if you discover you are spending $3,000 more per month than you are taking in, that is when you need to look at where your money is going. You want to be in a strong financial position, with plenty of cushion, as you move into the future.

Often, people who are spending more than they bring in are running up credit card debt or making withdrawals from savings accounts. That type of deficit is not sustainable.

People often expect their expenses in retirement to be similar to the expenses they have while they are still working. Other people anticipate spending less money. It is rare that people will spend *more* money in retirement.

Again, we would much rather err on the side of caution. For this reason, we will use current expenses to extrapolate the amount you will need in retirement, even if you think you might spend less once retired. I believe this is more of an art than a science. Again, having some cushion—some margin—will ease the impact of unexpected situations that can arise in the future. Those often manifest as an economic downturn, a personal emergency, or premature loss of your income.

Recently, I was at a meeting of almost thirty advisors at Carson Group headquarters. As we worked with the financial-planning tool we use, every single advisor in that room, at one point or another, said most of their clients have no idea how much they spend each month. Plus, they agreed that people who do try to estimate their spending tend to underestimate the amount significantly.

I agree. I would say only 10 to 20 percent of the families we serve truly know how much they spend. Once they begin using a budget, they gain discipline in their spending and saving.

When we build your personal financial plan, as mentioned, we need to know where you are now. Then we can figure out how to move you from that point to where you want to be in the future. Knowing your assets and expenditures is our starting point, our foundation, for your plan. If we don't know where you stand, we cannot design a financial plan that will be a meaningful guide for your future.

> **I would say only 10 to 20 percent of the families we serve truly know how much they spend. Once they begin using a budget, they gain discipline in their spending and saving.**

No One Budgets to the Exact Dollar

Another aspect of budgeting that scares people away is the assumption that they have to account for every single dollar they spend. I don't know anyone, including myself, who can account for every single dollar that comes in and goes out. It's virtually impossible because from year to year, expenses change.

In essence, budgeting is just a mindfulness exercise. It's a tool you can use to see where your money is going and to see if your expenses align with your goals. Look at every expense through a lens of, "Is this something I need?" What you continue to spend money on and what you discontinue is a personal decision that you need to make.

A budget is your first step in building a plan that aligns your spending with your true priorities.

We Need an Accurate Picture of Your Actual Spending to Build Your Plan

As mentioned, most people spend either the same in retirement as they do before, or less than that. It is rare for people to increase their spending in retirement. A couple who tends to spend $100,000 per year isn't likely to begin spending $150,000 per year once they retire.

One couple I have been building a retirement plan for recently told me they will need about $75,000 per year of income in retirement. I knew, simply from reviewing their tax returns, investment statements, and other documents that they were spending more than that. They were spending at least $75,000 plus regular withdrawals totaling $20,000 to $30,000 per year from their investment accounts. When I mentioned that to them, they said, "No, that isn't right. We've rechecked our annual expenses, and it's no more than $75,000."

Because people's current spending is a good gauge for future spending, it is of paramount importance that we have an accurate number to use as our starting point. I wanted to make sure we had an accurate assessment of this couple's actual spending. So I showed them all their numbers, which added up to almost $100,000 in expenditures per year. They were stunned. They had no idea they were spending that much.

The math doesn't lie.

There was a bit of finger pointing, with the spouses claiming the other one must be responsible for the excess spending. This is one reason it is critical for spouses or partners to be honest and transparent with one another about their finances. We need at least one person in a couple to have a good handle on their financial situation. In this case, it seemed that neither spouse had a good handle on their situation. They both looked pretty confused!

One issue is that one of the spouses has friends who are at a higher financial level than they are. They were attempting to enjoy life to the same extent that their friends were, but it just wasn't possible because their income was significantly less than the other couple's.

This huge gap between their perceived and actual spending would have led to a significant shortfall later, during their retirement years.

For example, if we had calculated their retirement at 20 years based on their estimated amount of spending, $75,000 per year X 20 years totals $1.5 million. But when we make that same calculation based on their actual spending—$100,000 for each of 20 years—that's a total of $2 million. That gap of $500,000 is significant. Their deficit would have been difficult for them to manage, especially considering that these were preliminary numbers, before we had even accounted for inflation. This couple would have realized, after they had already stopped earning incomes, that they needed to cut back on their spending significantly.

Again, the entire process of setting a budget and following it is a powerful exercise—both in awareness and also in discipline. Once you get past the discomfort associated with discovering where you really stand, you will find it empowering to manage your spending in a way that is conducive to reaching your future goals.

We Rarely See Our Money Anymore

Advances in technology have changed the way we interact with money. Decades ago, people cashed their paychecks at the bank and then paid their bills in cash. Because the currency was tangible, they could count it at any given moment to know how much money they had.

Back then, it was common for people to divide their cash into envelopes, labeled with various categories of spending, such as "Mortgage/Rent," "Utilities," and "Groceries." They would determine how much they could, and would, spend in each category. When the money in an envelope was gone, they could not, and would not, spend any more money in that category.

Times have changed a lot. Today, we rarely see our money. Our income is typically deposited automatically, and many of our expenses are paid or withdrawn automatically. We don't see cash unless we make an ATM withdrawal. Plus, many people use various apps and software to help them manage and budget their money.

It can be difficult to know how much we have at any time. I know quite a few people whose method of budgeting is to see how much money is left in their accounts once they have paid all their bills. That is not budgeting!

Back when people used checks to pay for everything, we kept a running tally of the amount in our checking accounts. When we wrote a check, we deducted that amount from the balance, resulting in a new balance. And then, when we received our bank statement each month, we would "balance the checkbook"—reconcile our check register with that statement and look for discrepancies. That checkbook register, which is now ancient history, played a valuable role in keeping us on track—it gave us a visual, easy-to-see picture of how much money we had in our checking account at any given moment.

Gen Z Has Revived an Age-Old Budgeting Strategy

However, an interesting trend has been taking place, particularly among Gen Z (those born between 1997 and 2012). They are using that same old-fashioned, yet extremely effective, envelope system, only today, it's called "cash stuffing."

So, why would these digital natives who've grown up with technology use such an old-fashioned method of budgeting?

According to *Forbes*, Gen Z have grown up during some tough economic times. They've seen their parents weather a massive recession and have endured a pandemic, and they are being careful with their money. This strategy gained renewed fervor as influencers on TikTok demonstrated how to divide your income into physical envelopes marked for different expense categories and then stuffing them with money.[6]

Using envelopes is an extremely effective budgeting strategy because you can easily see when the money you set aside for a category, such as groceries, is dwindling. At that point, you know to start cutting back. This method reinforces the psychology behind budgeting.

---

6. "Cash Stuffing: What It Is and Why It's So Popular With Gen Z," Jordan Rosenfeld, GOBankingRates, May 16, 2022, https://www.gobankingrates.com/money/financial-planning/cash-stuffing-what-it-is-why-so-popular-with-gen-z/.

My father-in-law uses the cash-stuffing concept when he goes to the casinos in Las Vegas. He is a very disciplined guy. He enjoys playing the slot machines and a poker-based table card game called "Let It Ride," but, like everyone else, he does not enjoy losing a lot of money. To help mitigate his losses and to keep his winnings as he resets for the next day, he allots himself money for each day of the week at the beginning of the trip and splits up that money into envelopes for each day he's going to gamble. He will take the envelope out for a given day and use it at the casino. At the end of the night, he puts away the envelope. If he didn't win, the envelope for that day might be empty. If he did win, then he will put those winnings into the envelope at the end of that day.

He is mitigating his potential downside; he knows in advance what his maximum risk will be. It's a very disciplined approach to allocating money toward something that brings him joy.

If you haven't found an effective way to budget your money, you might want to try cash stuffing!

Start the Budgeting Habit as Early as Possible

If you do not pick up the habit of budgeting from an early age, it is difficult to develop it as a positive habit. Sometimes, people think that because they're just out of college and their expenses are pretty straightforward, they don't need to budget. However, it's great to establish the budgeting habit while your expenses are less complicated so you will continue to budget as your finances become more complex.

There is no need to overthink this; a budget doesn't have to be complicated. It's really a matter of keeping an eye on how much you spend each month, and on what, and then compare that with the amount you're bringing in. Then it's easy to adjust your spending to ensure you have enough money for your current expenses, as well as money to save for the future.

Knowing what your budget is will make it easier for us to build a personal financial plan for you.

> **It's great to establish the budgeting habit while your expenses are less complicated so you will continue to budget as your finances become more complex.**

Develop the Positive Habit of Tracking Your Spending

You can discover your actual expenses rather easily. Many banks and credit card companies offer automated analyses of your spending in key categories, based on the nature of your transactions. You can use those reports as a starting point. Or you can create a list of your own spending categories and create an Excel spreadsheet on which you track all your expenditures.

This is a big step to understanding where your money is going and what is important to you and your family. Like any other positive life change, creating and following a budget is a good habit that needs to be developed over time. Keep in mind that the budget you build today most likely will not look the same two, five, or ten years from now. Your priorities will change, and you will need to adjust your budget to reflect those shifts.

Resources to Guide You in Budgeting for Your Family

Because budgeting is such a personal exercise, different strategies work for different people. As long as you are doing something to budget your money, it doesn't matter if you use the no-tech "cash stuffing" method we discussed—placing a certain amount of cash in envelopes earmarked for different categories of spending—or high-tech strategies such as apps and software.

Here are some specific resources you might want to consider as you develop your budgeting habit.

1. Our White Paper, The Family Budget

Managing family finances has become more complex than ever as the economy, job market, and family structures have undergone dramatic changes in recent years. We provide the families we serve with a copy of our white paper, *The Family Budget: Helping You Find Your Freedom*, to simplify the process of budgeting.[7]

2. Business Software

For many years, *businesses* have relied on QuickBooks® and other software programs and apps to document, track, and analyze their financial situations. Why not use these same tools to guide *your family's* spending? Creating a profit and loss (P&L) statement will be just as useful for your family as it is for a business.

3. Bank and Credit Card Spending Reports

Take advantage of the service your bank and credit card companies provide—coding their customers' expenditures into categories and providing an end-of-year statement of how much they have spent for the past year in each category. If you do not already have access to these reports, ask about them. They will give you at least a high-level overview of what's coming in and what's going out.

You can take this one step further and create your own Excel spreadsheet. Include all the spending categories (mortgage/rent, utilities, groceries, eating

---

7. You can download a free copy of our book, *The Family Budget: Helping You Find Your Freedom*, at https://cloud.carsonmx.com/re-source?brandid=0016g00000bSHiFAAW&guidekey=family-budget.

out, clothing, etc.) on the spreadsheet, and keep track of your spending from your debit and credit cards. Then add your income to the same spreadsheet, and compare your annual spending with your annual income. If there is a gap, work with your spouse, if applicable, to decide where to cut back.

When you are planning your future and prioritizing those things that bring you joy, you want to make the most of your income-earning years so you can have the best retirement possible. The more money you save now, the more you will have later. Curbing your spending enables you to save more. So, once you know what your goals are for the future, we can prepare a plan that helps you get there in the quickest way possible. As always, we err on the side of caution because unexpected expenses and costs, such as inflation, can leave you with less money than you expected.

I encourage you to view your budget not as a "dirty word" or a burden, but as your own personal tool to help you save for the most joy-filled retirement.

Chapter 3—Making It Personal

1. What brings you joy in life? What expenses do you consider must-haves? Build your budget around those priorities, and then consider reducing your spending in other areas. Do not feel guilty about spending your hard-earned money on the things that matter most to you. And don't let anyone else spend-shame you, either.

2. How closely do you follow your spending? If you have not done so, use automatic reports from your bank and credit card companies to identify how much money you spend in various categories per year. Or create your own Excel spreadsheet, and document your expenditures from your checking account and credit cards. Then compare the amount you spend with the amount you're bringing in.

3. Identify areas where you can cut back on your spending. This includes products or services you don't even need or want, such as online or magazine subscriptions.

4. Think of a budget not as an imposition or intrusion into your privacy, but rather as a powerful tool to help you reach your financial goals faster. Awareness is the first step.

5. What did you do today that brought you joy? [®]

Use a Side Hustle to Reach Your Goals Faster

Side hustles are more prevalent than ever. The disruption that COVID-19 created in our lives generated an unprecedented interest in starting businesses, either to replace former W-2 jobs or to supplement them.

A survey The Harris Poll conducted in May 2022 revealed that 40 percent of Americans had a side hustle, up from 34 percent in December 2020. They were spending an average of 13.4 hours per week working on their side hustles; 44 percent said they spent less than 10 hours per week in those ventures. Americans who had a side hustle at that time were making, on average, $12,689 per year from it.[8]

Chances are, you have a hobby and/or talents you enjoy a lot and could turn into a business.

8. "Zapier Report: 40% of Americans Have a Side Hustle in 2022," Zapier, June 7, 2022, https://zapier.com/blog/side-hustle-report-2022/.

Why Side Hustles Are Appealing

I see two major reasons why people create side hustles:

1. **The financial aspect.** Many people start side hustles to create additional cash flow for their households. This extra income often enables people to enjoy vacations, hobbies, and other activities they cannot support solely with their regular jobs.

2. **The personal-fulfillment aspect.** I've seen many people start side hustles because after years in the workforce, they finally realize what they are passionate about and enjoy (and it's not the full-time job!). This aspect of side hustles isn't discussed much.

   Many people go to college right out of high school. They choose a major that seems right to them at the time. Once they complete their degrees, they get jobs in the fields they studied. Once they begin working in those professions, they often realize, "This isn't what I want to do for the rest of my life." It might be 5, 10, 15, or more years after college that they discover something else they would like to do. Some people begin a side hustle to find out if it might be worth switching careers at some point;

others have no plans to quit their day jobs and continue to pursue both their regular jobs and their side hustles.

Whether they end up switching careers completely or not, the side hustle revives their enthusiasm in what they are doing while helping them financially. The side hustle allows them to ease into the potential transition without the pressure of having to make the switch right away. It gives them time to explore their options.

Shark Tank Led the Way

Eleven years before the COVID-19 pandemic changed the workforce, *Shark Tank* debuted on ABC in August 2009. On this series, ambitious entrepreneurs from all walks of life present their business concepts to the "sharks"—wealthy venture capitalists—with the hope that at least one of them will see the merits of their ideas and invest in them.

This is sort of a chicken-and-egg question: Which came first—the side hustle or *Shark Tank*? Either way, the show has led more people than ever to consider side hustles more seriously. It has given people a forum where they can present their ideas and, even if they don't receive funding, to at least get valuable feedback for strengthening the marketability of their ideas.

Many of the people who have experienced overwhelming success on *Shark Tank* were working in unrelated full-time careers when they started their side hustles. Some of the most successful ventures aim to solve a common problem a lot of people encounter.

I believe the show encapsulates the entrepreneurial spirit of our country. It allows people to consider a different option than the usual college-to-career path and to pursue their passions, rather than settling for a steady paycheck that offers little fulfillment.

By the way, there are many *Shark Tank*-inspired products in the Sprung home. Please feel free to ask me which ones!

Many of the people who have experienced overwhelming success on *Shark Tank* were working in unrelated full-time careers when they started their side hustles.

Business Lessons I Learned from My Dad

Earlier, I said my dad was a New York City schoolteacher and had a second job. Back then, they didn't call it a "side hustle."

To help pay the bills for our family, he established a company called Larmel Foods. He created his company name the same way I created mine—by combining two family names. He combined the first three letters of my name, "Lar," with the first three letters of my sister

Melissa's name, "Mel," to form "Larmel."

He sold packaged snacks to college bookstores and small grocery stores. He would buy candy, fruit, nut mixes, and trail mixes and combine them as variety packages.

Sometimes, he taught college while also teaching high school, so there were times when he was actually working three jobs.

My dad never had to *tell* me the importance of a strong work ethic—he *showed* me. Watching him work hard inspired me to want to do the same. When I wasn't at school, I used to go with him to visit his customers. We would see which products they were running low on and fill their shelves. We would load up the car in the morning, and by the end of the day, when we got home, it was empty.

One year when I was in college, I was looking to do some summer work. I went to him and said, "Hey, Dad, let me go out and try to get you more accounts. Let me spend the summer trying to increase your number of accounts and hopefully increase the amount of product you're delivering. That will increase your revenue, which will hopefully help your profit over the course of the year. Let me help out the family."

I figured he would be thrilled to hear my idea. But he said, "That's all well and good. While you're home for the summer, you can help me deliver all those orders. But once you go back to school, I won't be able to take care of all that myself. Larry, if you increase my business by 25 percent, I won't be able to sustain that through the school year."

That taught me to think about how businesses run—about capacity and the importance of planning for growth. Because one person can only do so much, especially when working one or two other jobs, entrepreneurs have to invest either in more people or in more opportunities to grow the company. But my dad was satisfied with the amount of business he was doing. It gave him the amount of extra income he needed.

Since then, I have been very mindful of the fact that, from a business perspective, you can't just think about growing a business; you also have to plan how you will continue to maintain and service the increased amount of business.

A Caution About "Plan B"

In our culture, we typically applaud people's ability to regroup when plans don't work out as expected—they move from "Plan A" to "Plan B." However, I want to caution you about relying on Plan B.

I don't think many people want to fit into the category of "jack of all trades, master of none." Yes, it's great to know a little bit about a lot of things, but typically, becoming an expert in one specific area is a more profitable and fulfilling outcome. For this reason, I recommend finding, and then pursuing, the one endeavor you excel at and enjoy most.

My view is that when people have a Plan B in mind already, it can prevent them from making a 100 percent commitment to Plan A. In other words, having a Plan B ready to put into action kind of gives you an "out" from Plan A. You can juggle both for a while, but in the long term, it's difficult to split your attention between your regular job and your side hustle effectively. You're not giving all your attention to either venture.

> **When people have a Plan B in mind already, it can prevent them from making a 100 percent commitment to Plan A.**

That can cause you to experience lackluster results in one or both of them.

At some point, you have to make a decision. You need to either commit to continuing your full-time job and pursue the side hustle as more of a hobby than an entrepreneurial venture, or you have to leave your regular job and focus 1,000 percent on the side hustle. Not many people can do both successfully over a long period of time. To help figure out which path is right for you, ask yourself, "Which venture brings me more joy?"

How Your Side Hustle Fits into Your Personal Financial Plan

Again, your personal financial plan, prepared for you by a competent, compassionate, fiduciary financial advisor, will guide every financial decision you make. Having that plan in place is vital to every aspect of our financial lives.

If you are thinking about quitting your full-time job to devote all your focus to your side hustle, your plan will guide you in replacing your W-2 salary and benefits in a way that ensures you and your family can live a comparable lifestyle after you quit. You want your new income stream to be at least comparable to your former one.

Preparing to commit to a side hustle will look different for everyone.

Your communication with your fiduciary advisor is of utmost importance. To guide you appropriately, he or she needs to know what you want to accomplish through the side hustle—your "why." This is much easier if you've already been working with an advisor; then it's a matter of simply adjusting your financial plan in light of your new goal.

Knowing where you stand and what you want to achieve with the side hustle, your advisor will guide you in setting up your business in a way that makes the most sense for you. For example, your advisor might tell you, "You have a sufficient amount of money saved in your emergency fund. Let's pull back a little on your retirement savings so you can save up your start-up capital for your side hustle." Again, this will differ for everyone.

You want your advisor to understand your ultimate goal and your desired outcome. This requires open, honest communication.

Without the guidance of an advisor, people run the risk of making financial moves that set them back. For example, if you dip into your emergency fund to start a side hustle, and then you need a major car or home repair, where will you get the money to cover that? Working with an advisor helps you plan your side hustle intentionally, methodically, and as part of your overall financial plan.

Some side hustles require no start-up capital, but others do. If yours falls into the second category, I recommend setting up a bank account for this expense and then depositing money into the account as you're able—without dipping into your emergency fund or retirement accounts. Make sure you have the financial wherewithal to make that leap from your full-time job to the side hustle *before* you do it.

There are general rules of thumb for the amount of money you need to set aside for your new venture, but I'm not a big fan of general rules because everyone's situation is different. Also, some people are ultraconservative and cautious in their approach, while others are comfortable taking on more risk.

After researching what it will require to launch your side hustle into a business, come up with a number you feel comfortable with, and work on saving that amount before you make the switch. We will guide you, but you need to feel comfortable with your approach as you launch your business and grow it over time.

Just as your personal financial plan keeps you on track to reach your goals with a full-time job, it will also help you stay on track as you build your side hustle into a new business—before and during your launch.

It Often Takes a Team to Cover All the Bases

One of the key themes of this book is the importance of making sure you have the right team in place to optimize the benefits of having and following a personal financial plan. This is true with side hustles as well.

If you have a side hustle in addition to your normal employment, it is important to let your advisor know so he or she can make sure your CPA is aware of the income being generated through your side hustle. You need to know how this income could affect your taxes, whether you need to set aside some money for those taxes, and whether you need to make quarterly tax payments. Unless your advisor is also a CPA, that information should be coming directly from your CPA.

If you typically prepare your own taxes, please be aware that your tax situation will get a bit more complicated once you start a side hustle. For this reason, I recommend that you hire a CPA to guide you on how to handle the taxes that are associated with the side hustle.

We often work with other professionals, such as CPAs and tax attorneys, to guide the families we serve in optimizing their financial situations. For example, the new income from your side hustle could put you in a higher tax bracket. It's important to work with your professional team to figure out the tax implications of your side-hustle income and avoid an unnecessary tax burden. (We discuss taxes more in chapter 9, "Taxes Affect Every Financial Decision.")

If you typically prepare your own taxes, please be aware that your tax situation will get a bit more complicated once you start a side hustle.

Some businesses require a legal structure before they can be established, and some require adherence to local, state, and/or federal regulations. In those cases, we work with attorneys and other professionals to ensure we're covering all your bases.

For example, if you establish a business that involves preparing and selling food, you will need to follow the guidelines required for such a business in your area. Also, we will work with other experts to guide you in protecting your personal assets once you establish a business. In many cases, this involves forming a company to transfer risk of being sued, for example, to your business so your personal assets are protected.

We work with a lot of authors. Some, before we met them, had written books and then, all of a sudden, earned $200,000 in royalties. They were so excited that they bought new cars or homes with cash. Next thing you know, they owed taxes on that income, but they were unable to pay them because all their money was tied up in their new purchases.

For many people who have always been W-2 employees, this is a whole new world. They do not realize that such payments from 1099 income have no taxes withheld. We ensure that they prepare for this unexpected expense so they are not blindsided at tax time.

Your financial advisor will help you plan and prepare for the ripple effects of your side-hustle income. Planning for your "happily ever after" requires thoughtful conversations about this extra income and how the increased cash flow might change your retirement planning options. It often requires a team approach.

The more complex your side hustle is, the more guidance you will need from a team of experts. It's important to get this advice in the planning stages, before you actually launch your side hustle as a business.

An Added Benefit to a Side Hustle: Teaching Your Children to Work and Save

Whether you have a side hustle or you are self-employed, you have a great opportunity to get your children involved in your business, once they are old enough.

Whether your children work in your business or at the neighborhood pizza shop, it gives you a great opportunity to educate them about putting money away for retirement. As soon as your kids generate earned income, they are eligible to open a Roth IRA or a traditional IRA and start saving.

If your children work for you, you will need to put them on the books and issue each of them a W-2. If you are not a business owner and your children work in an outside business, they will receive W-2 forms from those companies. Either way, this is an excellent way to introduce them to the importance of saving money at an early age.

The law varies by state in terms of the age at which children can legally begin working. I suggest that you check with your state and local governments to find out what the rules are in your area. Where we are located, most kids can get working papers at the age of 14.

Both of my kids have worked in some way, shape, or form since the age of 14. They both have their own

Roth IRAs and have been contributing to them on a regular basis since then.

Introducing your children to the value of work and saving early on really helps set them up for success.

Pursue Your True Passion

In my experience, the people who have the most success in turning side hustles into businesses are those who pursue their true passion. Plenty of people start businesses simply because they think they will generate a lot of income. But if those ventures are not personally fulfilling, their enthusiasm can wane over time. In essence, they're simply adding another job to the mix or replacing one job with another.

Figuring this out requires an internal look at yourself. What do you already enjoy? What things are you doing today that you could potentially turn into a side hustle, to generate both joy and additional income in your life?

I encourage you to pursue a side hustle that you love so much, you can't wait to begin each day working on it. Here are two examples of what that can look like:

1. A woman who caters meals for our firm has an unrelated full-time job, but she loves cooking and enjoys catering on the side. She's an awesome cook. She prepares the meals in the

early morning and then delivers them to us and other clients during her lunch break from her job. We love ordering from her.

2. One of the people we work with is a talented photographer. Over time, she began specializing in pre- and post-birth family photography. She has turned her passion for photography into a thriving business in which she creates professional portraits of women right before they give birth and after the babies are born, with their husbands and other children. She is passionate about memorializing and honoring this significant milestone in people's lives.

Successful side hustles like these typically begin organically, as activities people love. It's easy to see how these can develop into full-fledged businesses.

Let's say I, like the client I just described, really enjoy photography. I enjoy taking photos and editing them online. I like seeing the joy on people's faces when they see high-quality photos that have captured happy moments in their lives. Word gets out, and before long, people I know begin contacting me to ask if I will photograph their weddings, client events, or bar mitzvahs. From there, my side hustle becomes a business I enjoy thoroughly. This is often how people build their passions into businesses.

Again, I recommend starting with your passion,

not with a dollar figure you need. So, instead of trying to figure out the fastest way to bring in $1,000, figure out how you can turn your interests and talents into a business that helps people solve problems and brings in additional income. Then work with your advisor to figure out the metrics.

Again, it's not about the money. It's about what brings joy into your life. Let passion drive your side hustle, and the money will follow.

> **Let passion drive your side hustle, and the money will follow.**

The Metrics Matter

Although I recommend starting your business based on your passion, obviously, you do need to figure out the metrics related to your side hustle so you can manage it more easily.

Earlier, I described how working with my father taught me a valuable lesson about capacity. How many hours can you devote comfortably to your side hustle? Your answer will determine the amount of time and energy you devote to it. Most businesses aren't profitable right away. Have a strong enough financial foundation that you can take your time getting the business launched and profitable. This is another reason it's imperative that you pick something you love. If you love it, you will be more likely to stick with it and continue to persevere, even during the tough times.

To calculate your company's profit, just subtract all your expenses from the revenue it generates. If your answer is a positive number, you've made a profit. If it's a negative number, you've experienced a loss. And if the answer is zero, your business is breaking even. Work with your financial advisor to do a break-even analysis before you launch your new business. This will help determine how much revenue your business needs to bring in to cover your expenses and how long it will take to become profitable.

> **Work with your financial advisor to do a break-even analysis before you launch your new business.**

Statistics vary, but many business analysts estimate that it typically takes a startup business two to three years to begin making a profit.[9] This time frame varies a lot according to factors such as the sector your business operates in, your start-up costs, and the number of customers or clients you can serve.

Three Ways to Apply Your Side-Hustle Income

There are several ways your side-hustle income can benefit you and your family. Here are three.

---

9. "How Long Does It Take for the Average Small Business to Turn a Profit?" GOBankingRates.com, date unknown, https://www.gobankingrates.com/money/business/how-long-does-it-take-for-the-average-small-business-to-turn-a-profit/.

1. **Close the gap between your current salary and your monthly expenses.** A side hustle can help you meet your family's basic financial obligations. The freelance caterer I just mentioned turned her passion for cooking into a side business when she got divorced and became a single mom. Your side hustle can close that gap so you can continue to enjoy the lifestyle you're accustomed to.

2. **Pay for "extras."** Maybe your family's income is meeting all the basic needs, but there's little or no money left over to enjoy your favorite things. Your side hustle can fund hobbies, vacations, home improvements, or other activities like joining a golf club or boating club.

3. **Reach your retirement goals faster.** Some people contribute a good portion of, or all, the money they bring in from side hustles to their retirement savings. Doing this makes it easier to max out your individual retirement account (IRA) or your 401(k) account through your employer, for example, without having to cut back on expenses.

In some cases, side hustles enable people to benefit in all these ways. This extra income creates more options than you had before.

Decades ago, when people retired, they typically stopped working completely. That isn't always the case anymore. Many of the families we work with continue to do some type of work after they retire, whether they work part-time in their long-term jobs or start side hustles. They do this for the financial aspect as well as for personal fulfillment. Plus, more of our younger clients are exploring side hustles than in the past.

We enjoy partnering with families on the exciting journey of launching businesses that bring them joy—and extra income.

Chapter 4—Making It Personal

1. If you have launched a business based on a side hustle, did you choose that business based on the income potential or on your passion in life? To what extent did you receive counsel from financial and legal experts? What have you learned from the experience? What would you do differently?

2. If you have not turned a side hustle into a business but are considering doing so, what passions and talents in your life could you turn into a business? What do you enjoy doing that

could bring in extra income?

3. What is your "why" for starting a side hustle? What would it ultimately help you accomplish?

4. Work with a fiduciary advisor to build your personal financial plan and to adjust it over time, as your situation changes or the markets and economy change.

5. What did you do today that brought you joy?*

How to Plan for Retirement Financially—How Much Money Is Enough?

It's no surprise that questions about money dominate most retirement discussions. In the financial community at large, advisors tend to focus on the money, so consumers fall into the pattern of letting money drive their retirement planning—"How much money will I need before I retire? How much will I need for my big goal?" That's the topic we explore in this chapter.

As you read this chapter, think about the financial aspect of retirement in the context of the bigger picture. In chapter 8, I explain importance of the mental and social aspects of retirement. Retirement is more than just the numbers. A successful retirement requires advance planning to ensure a smooth transition in all aspects. And advance retirement planning leads to a greater capacity for joy in your life.

There Is No "Magic Amount" of Money You'll Need

When I was a kid, I remember hearing that if you had $1 million, that would be enough money to retire on.

There is no "magic" number, however; plus, the number is different for everyone. The amount you will need is a combination of the assets you have accumulated and the amount you are spending. For example, if two couples have the same amount of assets, but one couple spends $50,000 per year and the other couple spends $150,000 per year, that second couple will obviously need three times more money over the course of their retirement. Likewise, you will need a more sizable retirement fund if you retire at age 50 than you will if you retire at age 65. Another factor is whether or not you still have a mortgage.

The good news is, we're living longer. The bad news is, we're living longer.

One thing we do know, though, is that most people today will need more money in retirement than in past generations, partly because people are living longer now.

The good news is, we're living longer. The bad news is, we're living longer.

Decades ago, someone who retired at age 60 might be in retirement for 10 or 15 years. Now, with people living longer, we need to prepare to live in retirement for 20, 30, or more years. This is why, for most of the families we work with, we recommend that they wait as long as possible, up to age 70, to receive their Social Security benefits. We recommend that they wait until they (1) are no longer working or (2) reach their full retirement age. We don't know how long we're going to live, so we need to plan for a longer retirement—just in case.

There Is No "Magic Age" to Retire, Either

In the United States, there is a construct about retirement that isn't ideal, in my opinion.

Because the US Social Security Administration has a specific timeline for when each American can retire, based on "full retirement age" (FRA), many people focus on that age as the appropriate time to retire. Age 65 is a big marker for many Americans as well because that's the age at which we can claim Medicare to reduce the cost of health care.

The overriding sentiment tends to be that once we hit FRA, *then* we retire and get to enjoy life.

I think that's a backward view. First of all, if you're not enjoying your work, consider making some changes now so you can derive more fulfillment from your career. And second, make it a top priority to begin working with a financial advisor who will build your personal financial plan to guide you into the future. With that plan in place, and knowing what you want to accomplish in life, you can begin viewing work as just one component of what you do and who you are.

Many people, including CEOs and professional athletes, struggle to retire happily because they are unable to separate their personal identities from their legacies in business or sports.

I believe we should be enjoying life all along, whether or not we're working. We shouldn't have to work for 30, 40, or 50 years and then, all of a sudden, pump the brakes and say, "Now I'm done with work. *Now* I'm going to enjoy life!"

We have seen many people aim for that all-important FRA number and then suddenly stop working. For decades, they have worked, setting and reaching goals. And then, after they've been retired for three or six months, they take on part-time or even full-time jobs because they're bored. They did not anticipate the void they would feel in their lives once they were no longer striving to reach goals every day. They did nothing to replace that void in advance of retiring. They miss the social interaction and the mental challenges that work gave them.

Average life expectancy increased steadily over the past decades, although that hasn't been the case recently. In the United States, life expectancy increased from an average of 68 years in 1950 to 79 years in 2013.[10]

As of December 2022, the average life expectancy for an American was down to 76.4 years. This number decreased by more than seven months in 2021 and by 1.8 years in 2020. Because of the COVID-19 pandemic, drug overdoses, and other factors, this is the shortest life expectancy reported in nearly two decades.

Still, people are living much longer than decades ago. This means many people live in retirement much longer than in the past. Because retirement can extend for decades, I think we need to be more mindful about what we want out of life and enjoy life along the way. Whether or not we continue to work in retirement, planning is essential.

Half of Americans retire between the ages of 61 and 65, according to the Life Insurance and Marketing Research Association (LIMRA). More specifically, 69 percent of Americans retire by age 66, and roughly 51 percent retire between the ages of 61 and 65. By age 75, 89 percent of Americans have left the labor force.[11]

The COVID-19 pandemic led to unprecedented numbers of Americans leaving the workforce. That

10. "The Aging of America: A Changing Picture of Work and Retirement," Angela M. Antonelli, Georgetown University Center for Retirement Initiatives, March 2018, https://cri.georgetown.edu/the-aging-of-america-a-changing-picture-of-work-and-retirement/.
11. "What Age Do Most People Retire In America?" Financial Samurai, updated April 22, 2022, https://www.financialsamurai.com/age-people-retire-america/.

included millions of older Americans who retired fully. Yet before long, an estimated 1.5 million retirees reentered the US labor market between the spring of 2021 and the spring of 2022, according to an analysis of Labor Department data. Some workers said rising costs, and the inability to keep up while on a fixed income, factored heavily into their decisions.[12]

Returning to work became more appealing for many retirees as companies allowed remote work.

When we hear this news about retirees returning to work, the implication is that they need to continue working for financial reasons. That is true, but we know of many retirees who have continued working in retirement because they haven't figured out a way to fill that void, or they didn't prepare properly for the mental and social components of retirement. We address these issues when working with the families we serve, in addition to the financial aspects of retirement.

Avoid Relying on General Rules of Thumb

With just about any decision we make in life, most of us are likely to search online for general rules of thumb and guidance. This is true of many people who

12. "Millions Retired Early During the Pandemic. Many Are Now Returning to Work, New Data Shows," Abha Bhattarai, *The Washington Post,* updated May 6, 2022, https://www.washingtonpost.com/business/2022/05/05/retirement-jobs-work-inflation-medicare/.

are preparing to retire.

General rules of thumb can be interesting to read and consider, and they do give us a starting point for quick, back-of-a-napkin calculations. However, I always caution people that no general guideline can lead to an accurate estimate of how much money they will need to enjoy a comfortable retirement.

> **No general guideline can lead to an accurate estimate of how much money you will need to enjoy a comfortable retirement.**

For example, one rule of thumb is "the 4 percent rule." This general guideline suggests that retirees can withdraw from their retirement accounts an amount equal to 4 percent of those savings during the year they retire and then adjust for inflation each subsequent year for 30 years.

Guidelines like this certainly give you a place to start, but they do not consider the many variables that can affect your retirement needs. These include the amount you and your family spend, the assets you have set aside, and the amount of time you will continue to work before retiring. This is why a *personal financial plan*, tailored to your unique situation by a fiduciary financial advisor, is a critical tool in guiding you into retirement.

Start Planning as Early as Possible

It is indeed critical to plan your retirement in advance, with your vision and goals in mind, and then determine how much money you might need per year in retirement.

We want to make sure you enter retirement with a plan that will enable you to maintain the lifestyle you and your family enjoyed while you were working. Circumstances beyond our control, such as inflation and market downturns, cause retirees and pre-retirees to worry how those trends will affect their retirement income. This is another reason why it is important to get a personal financial plan in place—when markets shift, we can simply make adjustments instead of starting from square one.

The financial aspects of retirement—the "How much money is enough?" question—is indeed critical to your future because once you stop working, you switch from the *accumulation* of assets to the *distribution* of those assets to yourself. Many people get so wrapped up in their day-to-day lives that they don't start planning for retirement as early as they could. Waiting too long causes them to miss out on the benefits, such as the way compound interest grows money over time, they could derive from beginning earlier.

The earlier you begin planning your retirement, the more opportunities you have for success.

How Your Expenses Might Change

No one wants to experience a downgrade in lifestyle when they retire! Most of us want to maintain the same lifestyle in retirement that we did while we were still working, to the extent possible.

Let's say two families live next door to each other. One family spends $100,000 per year, and the other spends $200,000. Those two lifestyles will look very different.

Some people spend less in retirement than they did before; others spend more. The key is to examine the expenses you have before you retire and assess the extent to which those expenses might change once you retire.

Health care is the biggest expense most people have in retirement. In many cases, health care costs more during retirement than during the working years. One reason is that medical issues tend to arise as we age. Also, even though retirees can begin receiving Medicare at age 65, that program has limitations.

A 2022 Fidelity study found that the average 65-year-old male-female couple entering retirement should expect to spend $315,000 on medical costs (assuming enrollment in Medicare Parts A, B, and D). Just one year earlier, the previous version of the same study reported a cost of $300,000 for health-care costs for the same couple.[13]

That's a $15,000 increase in just one year! Given numbers like this, you can see why we like to err on the conservative side when we estimate retirement expenses. We want you to be prepared and not be blindsided by any surprises once you stop working.

The average cost is higher for women, largely because women have a slightly higher life expectancy than men. Fidelity reported that the average 65-year-old male should expect to spend $150,000 on healthcare costs throughout retirement, while the average 65-year-old woman should anticipate spending $165,000.[14] Of course averages are just a snapshot of the overall population, so your numbers will be different than other people's.

I recommend that you *overestimate* your expenses during retirement, just to be safe. Then back out of that total to determine the amount of money you might need to cover those expenses into and through retirement. Again, we will need to continue to monitor your personal financial plan and adjust it as unexpected shifts—economic, personal, and otherwise—arise.

---

13. "Fidelity: Average Couple Will Spend Over $300,000 on Health Care After Retirement," Maurie Backman, The Motley Fool, reported in *USA Today*, updated May 19, 2022, https://www.usatoday.com/story/money/personalfinance/retirement/2022/05/19/how-much-will-healthcare-cost-in-retirement-prepare-to-be-shocked/50245979/.
14. Ibid.

Your wishes for how you want to handle your finances is another huge variable when it comes to retirement expenses.

Some families want to pay off all their debt before they retire and then spend down all their assets to zero. In an ideal situation, the day they pass would be the day on which their bank account reaches zero. On the flip side, we have folks who say, "I want to set aside a certain amount of money to pass on to my children, grandchildren, and other heirs while also enjoying a comfortable retirement."

Whatever your wishes are, we include these priorities in your personal financial plan.

Inflation Is a Hungry Monster

We never know when inflation will increase, or by how much. But, like the markets and the economy, we can be sure inflation will fluctuate. Again, I like to plan for the worst-case scenario when estimating how much of a bite inflation will take out of your retirement savings.

The annual inflation rate for the United States was 9.1 percent for the 12 months that ended in June 2022. That is the highest rate since November 1981, according to the US Labor Department. On average, we see inflation of 2.5 to 3 percent per year.[15] Inflation can eat a sizable chunk of your retirement savings, so we must build this into your personal financial plan.

Let's say you are age 55 now, and you plan to retire in 10 years, at age 65. Your living expenses total about $100,000 per year. Because of inflation, that $100,000 will buy less in 10 years than it buys now. And that amount will buy even less 20, 30, or 40 years from now. Accounting for a reasonable rate of inflation when we build your personal financial plan will help you avoid a shortfall because of inflation down the road. Doing this adds a cushion, or buffer, to your plan.

> **Inflation can eat a sizable chunk of your retirement savings, so we must build this into your personal financial plan.**

The Importance of Having All Your Information on Your Advisor's Platform

A first step in the process of creating your personal financial plan is to get all your assets, financial information, and important documents in one place. Once you have provided us with everything we need, we will create your place in our highly secure online portal

---

15. "Current US Inflation Rates: 2000–2021," US Inflation Calculator, https://www.usinflationcalculator.com/inflation/current-inflation-rates/.

that you, and we, can access at any time.[16] We can link any and all accounts to your client portal, and they all feed into your personal financial plan. As your assets increase, decrease, or remain the same, we can get a real-time picture of where you stand.

Often, people call us to ask how a certain scenario might affect their retirement plans. Once all their information is in our system, it is easy for us to run some numbers using various "What if?" scenarios. We want your plan to be a dynamic guide that is always up-to-date and always accessible to you.

Our state-of-the-art technology eliminates the need for us to gather updated documents each quarter or year and load everything into the system again. Once your information is in our system and linked to the various sources, your personal financial plan is updated automatically.

Having everything in one place also makes it much easier for us to ensure that all details are the same across accounts. You might be surprised at the number of people who list different beneficiaries in their wills than they do in their retirement accounts. As you can

---

16. As a client of Mitlin Financial, you can simply go to our website at https://www.mitlinfinancial.com/ and click on "Client Login," located in the top right corner of your screen. Then, under the "Client Experience" subheading on the left side of the new web page, you can review your investment accounts, communicate with your team, and access our "Client Experience Optimizer" with just one click.

imagine, this can lead to unsavory outcomes, such as leaving money to an ex whom you forgot to remove from a set of paperwork.

On our platform, our portfolio strategy team makes capital market assumptions on a "go-forward" basis. Analyzing your unique set of data, they can assess how your portfolio might be affected based on the economy, the markets, inflation, and other factors. When our strategists feel that those projections are changing, they update them in our system, and all our clients' plans are updated automatically.

For example, if we had made projections based on 1 percent inflation, but then inflation was 3 percent, we will make that adjustment and analyze how it affects each client's portfolio. Then we make recommendations, if necessary, to compensate for the new projection.

This is why sometimes, your projection, which we call your "success rate," will change, even if your assets and your time horizon before retirement didn't change. Your success rate will decrease if inflation rises. Your success rate can increase, as well, when factors work in your favor—such as inflation decreasing, for example.

Again, our platform makes it easy to investigate different scenarios. You might tell me, "Larry, I'm worried that inflation might rise to four percent. What would my situation look like if that's the case?" We can find out in an instant, thanks to the technology we use.

Communicate with Your Fiduciary Advisor Regularly

One of the most valuable benefits of establishing a long-term relationship with your fiduciary advisor is your ability to receive ongoing advice. Communicating with your advisor and other professionals is extremely important in making the most of your personal financial plan.

I think about how I would want my advisor to communicate with me and what my expectations would be, from a communication standpoint, if I were in your

> **I think most people should expect to have at least have one annual meeting with their advisor.**

shoes. I think most people should expect to have at least have one annual meeting with their advisor. There can be, and often are, more meetings than that.

In addition to that annual check-in, I believe most clients can benefit from periodic check-ins with regard to any changes in the family's financial or personal life situation. Families are busy doing what they do. Something may change. They may have to change jobs. Somebody may get ill. Sometimes they don't think to call their advisor when these situations arise, but those changes are pertinent pieces of information to the overall planning. So it's important for your advisor to check in with you on a regular basis to make sure that you're on the same page. He or she needs to be fully apprised of anything that's going on with the family.

There are other times when advisors need to communicate with clients. For example, if and when markets go awry, there should be communication between the advisor and the family. I believe advisors should contact their clients 10 to 12 times per year, at a minimum. Those communications can be in the form of phone calls, emails, texts, in-person meetings, or virtual meetings. Obviously, the family can reach out and communicate with the advisor if they feel they want or need more communication than that.

In some cases, clients prefer minimal communication with their advisors, for whatever reason. That's an important conversation with your advisor, to make sure he or she is communicating with you in the ways and at the level you prefer.

How We Communicate with the Families We Serve

We are constantly communicating with the families we serve. We want them to stay informed, and we want to reduce some of the anxiety that comes with unexpected shifts and changes in their situations.

One venue we use for doing that is through our weekly newsletter that we email to all the families we serve and to those who have opted in to receive our emails. The newsletter contains three main components, the first of which is a section called "Weekly Market Commentary." It's an overview of what happened the week before in the markets and how it may affect them. The second component of the newsletter is a section that summarizes the prior week's Mitlin Money Mindset™ episode. The third component is an educational resource, maybe a white paper or a webinar that we have coming up.

When there is a major shift in the market, we may send out an email addressing that.

In addition, our investment team conducts a quarterly market overview to assess what's going on in the markets, and we host a webinar to share that information.

Keeping everyone informed makes it easy for us to get in front of market downturns and other changes that can affect your portfolio. When the markets experience a downturn, it can be easy for people to panic, although we always advise staying put when the market shifts. Research shows that, throughout history, staying in the market is much wiser than bailing out of the market and getting back in again.

When the pandemic started to affect people financially, the Mitlin team called every single family we serve to answer their questions and assure them that we were controlling the aspects we could control and watching the aspects we could not control. At all times, we are keeping a close watch on every factor that impacts your personal financial plan—so you don't have to.

We want you to be aware of adjustments we are making to your plan, and why. Sometimes the adjustments can be significant, but most of the time, they are minor. However, sometimes, minor adjustments in your plan can lead to major improvements.

For example, in November 2021, it was apparent that the Federal Reserve was going to increase interest rates to try to reduce inflation. So, going into 2022, we knew there was a high likelihood that interest rates would rise soon. Our strategy team started working with the families we serve to make minor adjustments to their portfolios, in preparation for the higher interest rates.

I cannot stress enough the importance of staying the course, even when factors outside our control are affecting your portfolio. Trust your team to fine-tune your plan to better prepare you for what's coming. Be open to the adjustments we recommend, and always ask questions so you understand our approach.

One of our core values at Mitlin Financial is to review, question, and improve everything—always. Even though we have a highly effective process in place, we still look at everything we do and question, review, and improve it.

The better prepared we are, the better we can

serve your needs. And the better prepared you are, the more likely it is that retirement will be the best stage of your life.

Chapter 5—Making It Personal

1. What rules of thumb have you used in the past to calculate how much money you will need for retirement? We advise using rules of thumb only as a starting point as you begin to think about retirement. They do not take your personal situation and needs into account. Please work with your fiduciary financial advisor to build your personal financial plan.

2. Recognize that there is more to retirement than just the money aspect. Plan to optimize your emotional, social, and mental well-being in retirement as well.

3. How will you spend your time in retirement? To what extent will those activities give you a strong enough purpose to keep you fulfilled when you are no longer working? Consider as many options as you can think of, and do so well before you retire.

4. What did you do today that brought you joy?[*]

Save Early for College

Like every other aspect of personal financial planning, saving for a college education requires thoughtful planning well in advance of your need for the funds. Paying for a college education is, outside retirement, one of the most expensive goals people can have. As always, the bigger the expense, the more benefit you'll receive from planning.

Saving early for your children's college education helps your children (and you) avoid a potential pile of debt down the road. As I mentioned in chapter 1, I used this strategy with my own family.

The Heavy Burden of Student Debt

Our nation is drowning in college debt.

From 2009 to 2022, the average student-loan-debt balance grew by nearly 92 percent, according to Experian data. Student-loan-debt averages had the biggest year-over-year increase from summer 2012 to summer 2013, when they jumped nearly 10 percent.

For Americans who have student-loan debt, the average balance is nearly $40,000—second only to home mortgages when it comes to consumers' average debt balance.[17]

Many theories exist about the reason for the surge in student-loan debt. I believe there are three key reasons.

1. **Parents fail to set expectations with their children**—The first reason is a scenario I describe later in this chapter, in which parents let their children decide where they want to go to college, based on their personal preferences. Many parents fail to set expectations with their children early on regarding what the parents will pay for and can afford. They don't want to disappoint their kids or say no to them, so they end up letting them attend schools they want, based on reasons that are unrelated to return on investment (ROI). Parents who don't set these expectations and ground rules early on with their children often end up paying inflated tuition that exceeds their budget and incurring debt.

2. **Some higher-education institutions promote the myth that everyone needs a college education**—Many universities are great at

17. "How Student Loan Debt Has Increased Over Time," Dom Di-Furio, Experian, August 24, 2022, https://www.experian.com/blogs/ask-experian/how-student-loan-debt-has-increased/.

marketing themselves. They have helped create a narrative that *all* students who graduate from high school should go to a four-year college or university and that such an education is essential for them to be successful in life.

I do not believe that narrative. Every student is different, based on his or her talents and aspirations, and many young people can derive tremendous value from going to a trade school or to a community college for a year or two. I believe it's important for young people, just as it is for adults, to follow their passion and do what brings them joy.

> **Many young people can derive tremendous value from going to a trade school or to a community college for a year or two.**

We have one client whose son decided college wasn't for him. He went to trade school instead to learn to be an electrician. At only 19 years old, he was already working in a paid job as an electrician. He will likely earn a very good living. I don't believe everybody needs the four-year degree that is often promoted as the superior option.

Plus, many students who are right out of high school have no idea what type of career they want to pursue. Starting out with general studies at a community college gives them time to explore their options. Once they decide what they want to major in, then they can transfer to a four-year college. Students who start college right out of high school, with no career plan in mind, can end up attending college for five or six years. That is costly, and if you've budgeted for four years of college for your child, that extra year or two can, again, cause you or them to incur debt.

3. **It is easy to access student loans**—A third reason for the sky-high student-loan debt in this country, in my opinion, is the fact that government and private lenders lend money to people for higher education easily. I think, many times, it's almost too easy to get the money. Often, people take out the maximum amount of loans they can for a student's college education without thinking through what's actually best for the student or which path will lead to the highest ROI. As with any type of loan, just because you can get approved for a student loan doesn't mean it is the right personal financial decision for you.

As of August 2022, student-loan borrowers in the United States owed a collective total of nearly $1.75 trillion in federal and private student-loan debt, according to the Federal Reserve Bank of St. Louis.

Almost two-thirds (62 percent) of the class of 2019 graduated with student debt. The average balance owed for a bachelor's degree was $28,950 per graduate. The average balance owed was much higher for higher-education degrees—for example, $66,300 for an MBA loan, $71,000 for a graduate-school loan, $145,500 for a law-school loan, $201,490 for a medical-school loan, and $292,169 for a dental-school loan.[18]

Although the student-debt-reduction initiative from the federal government will ease the burden of some student-loan debt for families, it will contribute to this country's deficit. In turn, we the taxpayers will end up paying for that debt.

Forgiving up to $10,000 per borrower under Biden's income limits would add up to $519 billion to the federal deficit over the next decade, according to a Wharton study.[19]

Americans can lower student-loan debt by saving for college early and being more thoughtful about the type of education that will benefit their families and each student the most.

18. "Student Loan Debt Statistics: 2022," Anna Helhoski and Ryan Lane, nerdwallet, August 25, 2022, https://www.nerdwallet.com/article/loans/student-loans/student-loan-debt.
19. "Canceling Student Debt Isn't Free. Here's Who Pays For It," Kelly Anne Smith, Forbes Advisor, updated August 26, 2022, https://www.forbes.com/advisor/personal-finance/who-pays-for-student-loan-forgiveness/.

College Costs Leveled Out, After Steady Increases

The good news is that after rising significantly for several decades, the cost of a college education began to decrease during the COVID-19 pandemic, although not by much.

The estimated total cost to attend a college for one year is called "cost of attendance" (COA). This figure includes tuition and fees, room and board, books and supplies, transportation, and personal expenses. Need-based aid, merit aid, and scholarships can reduce a student's total cost.[20]

Between 1980 and 2020, the average price of tuition, fees, and room and board for an undergraduate degree increased 169 percent, according to the Georgetown University Center on Education and the Workforce. In 1980, the price to attend a four-year college full-time was $10,231 annually—including tuition, fees, and room and board, adjusted for inflation—according to the National Center for Education Statistics. By 2019–20, the total price increased to $28,775, representing an increase of 180 percent. The cost of a college education at a private nonprofit institution, on average, is more than double

20. "How Much Does College Cost?" CollegeData.com, date unknown, https://www.collegedata.com/resources/pay-your-way/whats-the-price-tag-for-a-college-education.

the cost of an education at a public college. In 2019–20, the average full-time student paid $48,965 at a private nonprofit college, compared to $21,035 at a public university.[21]

But then the average costs for college tuition and fees stayed about the same between September 2019 and early 2022, according to the US Bureau of Labor Statistics, even though inflation led to rising prices for all other goods and services. In fact, from the academic year 2019–20 to 2021–22, average tuition, fees, and room and board dropped 0.2 percent at private nonprofit four-year schools and dropped a further 1.7 percent from 2020–21 to 2021–22. Costs at public four-year schools followed a similar pattern in the same time frame.[22]

There isn't a strong consensus about the reasons for these increases and decreases. One possible reason is the changing availability of state and local funding for a given school. When public colleges receive less state and local funding, they often pass costs on to students in the form of increased tuition and/or fees.

21. "College Tuition Inflation: Compare the Cost of College Over Time," Brianna McGurran, *Forbes* Advisor, updated March 28, 2022, https://www.forbes.com/advisor/student-loans/college-tuition-inflation/.
22. Ibid.

A Gap Between Intention and Execution

Despite the fact that many people consider college education a top goal, many never follow through and actually put money aside for college. One reason for this gap between intention and execution is that people often reason that they can always borrow money for college, whereas they cannot borrow money for retirement. So they choose to save money for retirement and put less of an emphasis on college. The problem with this approach is that if you wait until your child is about to enroll in college to focus on funding, you lose the benefit of early saving and planning.

> **Despite the fact that many people consider college education a top goal, many never follow through and actually put money aside for college.**

Another reason people don't save for college is that the daunting cost of a college education often intimidates people so much that they end up doing nothing about it. A college education for two children could cost a total of a quarter of a million dollars, and for four children, that cost could exceed $500,000. The key to tackling this gargantuan expense is by simply envisioning a future in which your children's college education is partially or completely paid for well in advance and then bringing that vision to reality by saving regularly and early in some sort of college savings plan—the earlier, the better!

As with other types of savings, you can benefit from compound interest over time.

It can be tempting to anticipate that your children will get a "full ride" to college, via academic or sports scholarships. However, most students do not, so it is wise to save in advance for college. (If your children do get their higher education paid for, you have options for using the money you have saved, so it is never a wasted effort.)

Research shows that in 2020, 58 percent of families used either academic-based or need-based scholarships to help pay for college. Approximately $8.8 billion was awarded in need-based scholarships, but only 1.5 percent of high-school students receive a *full* scholarship. Just 7 percent of students are likely to receive a scholarship, and only 0.2 percent of students receive more than $25,000 in scholarships. The average amount used per scholarship was $7,923, and overall, scholarships and grants helped to pay for 19 percent of college costs.[23]

My Story

I never expect the families we serve to do something I would never do or have not done. Allow me to share with you my own personal story about saving early for college.

_____

23. "Scholarship Statistics," ThinkImpact, 2020, https://www.thinkimpact.com/scholarship-statistics/.

As I mentioned in chapter 1, I began saving money for my children's college education in a 529 plan in 1998—before Denise and I married and had children! Our first child wasn't born until 2003. Yet I knew I wanted to have children someday, and it was a priority for me to plan and save early for their college education. I envisioned my best life possible to include children and the ability to send them to any college of their choice.

When I started the plan, I named myself as the beneficiary and began adding money to the account on a regular basis. When our first child was born, I named him as the beneficiary to the plan, and when our second son was born, I opened a second account and named him as the beneficiary. Now, fast-forward to today, our older son is in college, and our younger son will be in college soon. We have accumulated significant monies in that plan, which we are now using to help pay for our first son's college education.

Because I started this plan early and benefited from compounding interest over time, only one-third of the account's value today is composed of contributions we've made. Approximately 70 percent of the value of our 529 account represents *growth* in the account over all those years. This means that only 30 cents of every dollar I am now using from that plan for my sons' education represents my money. All of that growth has accumulated, and because we're using the money for college education, we are taking the money out tax-free. That growth has never been taxed at all.

However, I did not save enough money in our 529 plan to fund 100 percent of our two sons' college education. I wanted to hedge my bets a little because I wasn't sure what the future would hold. The plan will cover most of their education, though. I encourage you not to worry about funding every penny of your child's college education. Starting early to save for even part of it will offset your expenses once your child enrolls in college. You will find it extremely helpful if you save for most of it.

My story shows you the power of starting a 529 plan very early on and adding regular contributions.

I started earlier than most. Few people have the foresight to set up a 529 plan before they even have kids! But doing so is a great way to save early for college. At the very least, I recommend establishing a 529 plan when you and your partner are expecting a child via birth or adoption.

A 529 Plan Is a Popular Option

Many people choose a 529 plan, as Denise and I did, because it is a tax-advantaged savings plan that can help you save on both the cost of education and your income taxes.

As you'll read in an upcoming section, 529 plans

aren't right for everyone, and there are alternatives. I am describing 529 plans here because that's the option we chose to save for our sons' college education.

One upside of 529 plans is that some of them show an average rate of return that's higher than what you would find with deposit accounts; however, growth of your money in a 529 plan is not guaranteed.[24]

Sometimes, people resist the idea of a 529 plan at first because their children have not expressed any interest in going to college. No worries—you can use a 529 plan at any eligible institution of higher education. That includes not only four-year colleges and universities but also qualifying two-year associate degree programs, trade schools, and vocational schools—both in the United States and abroad.

You also can use a 529 plan to pay for an education at a private high school. Please be aware of state laws and restrictions when doing so.

For example, in New York, if you withdraw money from a 529 plan to pay for private high school, you will avoid the federal tax, so that money will come out tax-free at the federal level. However, because the state of New York has not acknowledged this change, your withdrawals will not be tax-free at the state level. In some states, 529 withdrawals for private high schools are tax-free at both levels. These expenses for high

---

24. "Best 529 Plans," Megan Hanna, the balance, updated June 26, 2022, https://www.thebalance.com/best-529-plans-5092896.

school are always federally tax-free if they are qualified expenses, but they may or may not be state-tax-free. Please work with your fiduciary advisor to make sure you use the best strategy.

How New Legislation Has Eased the Rules for Using 529 Plans

The federal rules for how you can use funds from a state-administered 529 plan have changed through the years.

For example, the 2019 Setting Every Community Up for Retirement Enhancement (SECURE) Act, which focused primarily on retirement, also made several major changes to the 529 rules. One change is that now you can use proceeds from a 529 plan to pay off some student-loan debt for the account beneficiary or his or her siblings, up to a lifetime maximum of $10,000 per individual. Previously, student debt was not considered a qualified expense. Another change that took place in 2019 is that now you can use 529 funds to pay for the fees, books, supplies, and equipment required to participate in an apprenticeship program that is registered and

Now you can use proceeds from a 529 plan to pay off some student-loan debt for the account beneficiary or his or her siblings, up to a lifetime maximum of $10,000 per individual.

certified with the US Secretary of Labor.[25]

If you set money aside in a 529 plan and end up not being able to use that money for your child's education, you can change the beneficiary to another child or relative. You also have the option of using that money to fund your own return to school for a degree. But if you end up being unable to use that money for any type of educational expenses, you will pay a 10 percent penalty and federal income tax on the growth, but not the principal, that is attributable to that withdrawal from your 529 account.

These rules were pretty reasonable, but even so, many people found them burdensome. Plus, a significant amount of money ended up "stranded" in unused 529 plans because the account holders were unable to use that money as they had originally intended. The Investment Company Institute reported that at the end of 2021, there were nearly 15 million 529 accounts holding a total of $480 billion. That's an increase of 13.0 percent since year-end 2020. At the end of December 2021, savings plans held $452.6 billion, while prepaid plans accounted for another $27.8 billion.[26]

---

25. "How New Tax Changes Promote 529 Investments," Rebecca Lake, Investopedia, updated June 30, 2022, https://www.investopedia.com/personal-finance/how-new-tax-changes-promote-529-investments/.
26. "Release: 529 Plan Program Statistics," Investment Company Institute, March 30, 2022, https://www.ici.org/research/stats/529s/529s_21_q4.

To enable Americans to use that money to fund their retirement accounts, President Joe Biden signed a $1.7 trillion funding bill—the SECURE Act 2.0—in December 2022. A provision in the bill gives parents the option to make tax-free rollovers of up to $35,000 from 529 tuition savings plans to Roth IRAs. You can make this change at no cost *if your 529 plan is at least 15 years old.*[27]

That money from your 529 plan will go into the Roth IRA account of your 529 plan's beneficiary. If your child is the stated recipient, his or her retirement fund (not yours) will get boosted. The Roth IRA contribution cap determines the yearly transferrable amount. That limit was set at $6,500 in 2023, and people over 50 are allowed an extra $1,000 as a catch-up allowance. You cannot make rollovers on any contributions or earnings made in the past five years.[28]

Let's say the worst-case scenario happens—you save money in a 529 plan, but the child you saved the money for does not, or is not able to, pursue a higher education, and none of your other family members, or you, will use the money. You now have more options than ever for using the money you've saved in your 529 plan for other purposes. So please do not allow potential "What if?" scenarios to discourage you from investing in a 529 plan

27. "Americans Can Get Up to $35,000 from Stranded Savings—See if You're Eligible to Get Your Money Back," Josephine Fuller, *The US Sun*, updated January 11, 2023, https://www.the-sun.com/money/7106704/americans-stranded-savings-eligible-get-money-back/.
28. Ibid

if it could be beneficial to someone in your family.

Please note that the SECURE Act 2.0 is the largest retirement legislation since the original Secure Act hit in the late 2019. The new legislation will help Americans save for retirement, aid those who are in or nearing retirement, and incentivize small businesses to offer retirement plans.

The Act also made sweeping changes to required minimum distributions, with the most prudent change being that most non-spousal inherited retirement accounts are required to be withdrawn over 10 years rather than stretching distributions out to avoid heavy tax liabilities.

The major provisions of this bill break down into five basic categories: expanded savings opportunities, required minimum distribution changes, expanded Roth opportunities, emergency funding, and retirement plan provisions. You can read more about how the SECURE Act 2.0 could benefit you in one of our recent blog posts.[29]

---

29. "SECURE 2.0 Act Aims to Increase Retirement Savings for Americans," Jamie Hopkins, Mitlin Financial, December 27, 2022, https://www.mitlinfinancial.com/insights/blog/secure-2-0-act-aims-to-increase-retirement-savings-for-americans/.

A 529 Plan Isn't Ideal for Everyone

As mentioned, 529 plans are not the best choice for everyone. Here are two reasons why.

1. A 529 plan could affect your child's ability to receive need-based financial aid

One downside of a 529 plan is that if you save money in a 529 plan for your children, it can affect their ability to receive need-based financial aid (but it won't affect merit-based financial aid). Now, if the child's parents are high earners, this isn't likely to be an issue because they probably do not qualify for financial aid anyway.

A 529 plan established by a child's *grandparents* does not affect need-based financial aid, however. In other words, money set aside in a grandparent's 529 plan is not included in a grandchild's financial-aid calculation.

Money set aside in a grandparent's 529 plan is not included in a grandchild's financial-aid calculation.

If the child's grandparents are in a good financial position, it may make sense for them to establish the 529 plans on behalf of the grandchildren.

2. Some 529 plans do not offer an FDIC-insured option

Not all 529 plans are insured by the Federal Deposit Insurance Corporation (FDIC).

As of August 31, 2022, there were twenty-nine 529 savings plans that offered some form of a federally insured product, down from thirty-one in 2021. There are two types of FDIC-insured products held inside 529 plans: certificates of deposit (CDs) and savings accounts. Because they are backed by the full faith and credit of the US government (up to certain limits), FDIC-insured products are suitable for conservative investors who are interested in preserving capital without taking on excess risk.[30]

Potential Alternatives to a 529 Plan

It is important to work with your fiduciary advisor to select the option that's best for your family. Here are three alternatives to 529 plans.

1. An Investment Account

One alternative to a 529 plan that some of the families we work with choose for college savings is an investment account. Depending on your investment portfolio, a brokerage account might offer similar growth rates comparable to 529 plans. Also, there are

---

30. "New Study: FDIC-Insured 529 Plans," Kristen Kuchar, Saving for College website, October 25, 2022, https://www.savingforcol-lege.com/article/new-study-fdic-insured-529-plans.

no contribution limits with many brokerage accounts.[31] However, brokerage accounts do not offer the tax benefits that 529 plans do.

2. A Custodial Account

In addition to 529 plans, families can set up custodial accounts for their kids. The parents are the custodians, and the child is the minor. Depending on the state you live in, there is a certain age at which those assets will automatically become the minor's. It's called the "age of majority."

In New York State, for example, if you set up a custodial account for a child, those monies will become the child's at the age of 21. As long as that money is used for the child prior to him or her reaching age 21, it can be used on their behalf, so it can be used for college.

A disadvantage of this type of account is the fact that whatever money is there at the age of majority in your particular state becomes that child's money. So, if the child wants to use it to buy a car instead of paying

---

31. Unlike brokerage accounts, 529 plans do not have annual contribution limits. However, contributions to a 529 plan are considered "completed gifts" for federal tax purposes. In 2022, up to $16,000 per donor (up from $15,000 in 2021) per beneficiary qualified for the annual gift-tax exclusion. Contributions above $16,000 must be reported on IRS Form 709 and will count against a taxpayer's lifetime estate and gift-tax exemption amount ($12.06 million in 2022). See "Maximum 529 Plan Contribution Limits by State," Kathryn Flynn, SavingForCollege.com, March 29, 2022, https://www.savingforcollege.com/article/maximum-529-plan-con-tribution-limits-by-state.

tuition that year, he or she can do that because at that age of majority, it is their money.

A second potential disadvantage is that if the family feels the child might be eligible at some point for financial aid for college, they will expect one-third of the child's custodial account to be used toward the child's college education. If the money is in a parent's name, like the 529 plan is, it does not have that same impact on the financial-aid calculation. This is something to think about and discuss with your advisor.

3. A Non-Custodial Account in the Parents' Names

Another option parents have to a 529 plan is to open a non-qualified, non-retirement, non-custodial account in their names and use those funds and savings toward their child's college education.

The downside with this option is that if and when they start liquidating those funds to pay for college, they are going to have to pay taxes (capital gains) on the growth of those funds. They would not have to do so with a 529 plan. However, those funds in the non-qualified account don't have the same restrictions that are placed on a 529 plan.

Again, the dynamics change when the grandparents establish such plans. Whether it's a 529 plan, a custodial account, or a non-qualified account, grandparents can also set up these accounts on behalf of their grandchildren if they want to help pay for college and/or help them get a head start financially.

Other options are available as well, and what works for someone else's family might not be ideal for yours. Let your fiduciary advisor be your guide.

Set Expectations with Your Children Early

Beginning early to save for your children's college education is extremely important. Almost as important is a nonfinancial aspect of looking to the future—setting expectations with your children about what you and your spouse can pay for once they are making plans to attend college.

> **Begin those conversations early on with your children about what your expectations are and what you are and are not willing to pay for so everyone is on the same page.**

I recommend that you begin those conversations early on with your children about what your expectations are and what you are and are not willing to pay for so everyone is on the same page. This will enable you to reinforce those expectations over time.

For example, let's say you begin talking with your daughter

when she is in the eighth grade about her higher-education plans, and she agrees to attend an in-state college. Then, when she's in her junior year of high school, she comes to you and says, "I've decided I want to attend an out-of-state college because it has a fantastic volleyball team."

At that point, it will be much easier to revisit the past discussions you've had with your daughter than it would be to tell her once she's about to graduate from high school, for the first time, that you cannot afford the tuition for an out-of-state college. You can say, "Well, hold on. That was not the deal. We've been talking about this since you were in the eighth grade, and you said you understood that we were willing to contribute money for an in-state college. The college you want to attend will cost twice that amount. As a family, we cannot afford that. Plus, we have to save for your brothers' and sisters' college education. This isn't only about you."

We work with a couple who thought their son would go to an in-state university, but he ended up attending an out-of-state university, which cost significantly more. Then, about six months before school started, the dad lost his job. Two years in, when the son was about to start his junior year, his dad still had not found a job. The family was racking up debt and facing hardship—yet they never had a conversation about the situation.

None of us wants to disappoint our kids. However, we can all benefit from having open, honest communication throughout the journey with our children and having a trusted fiduciary advisor to consult about options.

Another family we work with also has two children, and they have been saving money for college for many years. One of their children is attending a university here in New York, and they have enough money set aside to cover his education. Their second child is attending an out-of-state university, and the amount they've saved will cover only about a year and a half of that child's education. This means the parents have to come up with the remaining two and a half years' worth of education. That's a hefty amount, considering that it costs about $70,000 per year for their child to attend that school. That is a significant shortfall. This out-of-state school does not have a unique program or specialized major that might have justified the extra spend.

If their younger child had gone to an in-state university, like their older one, they would have had enough to cover all the expenses related to both college degrees. The parents did not have these conversations with their children early on; if they had done so, they might have had a more manageable outcome.

View a College Education as a Potential Return on Investment

People tend to do more research and investigation into their automobile purchases than they do for their children's college education. In my opinion, this is one of the contributing factors to the crisis we are seeing in the United States related to college debt.

A lot of times, even when parents do their research, the decision about where their children will go to school is heavily dependent on what the children want to do and which school environments appeal to them.

In my view, a college education is a tool to get young people established in their careers. As such, I believe we need to view college through a lens of *potential return on investment* (ROI). You're making an investment in your child and his or her future.

As with any financial undertaking, every family is different. What's right for my family may not be right for yours. My wife and I discussed the type of planning we felt comfortable offering our sons. We told them we would offer both of them a fully paid education if they attended a state university. They would graduate with no college debt. Denise and I both came from the state university system. Neither one of us came out with one cent of debt, and we wanted our boys to have the same opportunity.

When our older son was about to graduate from

high school, he applied to some state universities here in New York, as well as some others. He found an out-of-state university that had a unique co-op program. Over the course of five years, he will get to complete paid six-month jobs with three different employers to help him experience what it would be like to work in each of those careers. Once he completes his degree, he will have real-life experience that he wouldn't receive in a traditional college program.

He came to us and said, "I get what you were saying about the state university, but I really feel that this school that I'm looking at, because of the co-op program, is going to put me in a better position post-graduation than if I went to a state university."

Denise and I looked at what the university offered, and the cost, and we talked with our son about it. We agreed that it was a good opportunity for him, and we felt like it had a potentially higher return on investment than an education from a state university. However, the program he was interested in cost almost twice as much.

We told him, "If you go to that school, we're going to need some help from you because you don't qualify for financial aid. You're going to have to work your tail off and get some scholarship money."

He did end up receiving scholarship money. As a result, he bridged some of the gap between the cost of the school he chose and a state university. Denise and I felt that the more costly program would result in a better ROI. We decided it would be worth spending the extra money each year because it made sense.

Denise and I felt that the more costly program would result in a better ROI. We decided it would be worth spending the extra money each year because it made sense.

Now, if our son had come to us and presented a different narrative, wanting to attend a more expensive university for reasons unrelated to potential ROI, we wouldn't have agreed to pay the extra cost. For example, if he liked a particular school because of the warm weather, the location, or the sports atmosphere, I assure you that my wife and I would have told him the additional $15,000 or $20,000 cost would be on his shoulders. We would have discouraged him from taking on that expense because then he would have graduated from college with some debt.

There are many different ways to save for a college education, but regardless of the one you choose, the key is to *begin saving early* and also to begin *setting expectations* with your children early. Again, please consult with your fiduciary advisor to find the best option for you and your family.

Chapter 6—Making It Personal

1. If you have children or plan to, but you have not focused on their college education yet, meet with a fiduciary advisor to begin saving and planning early.
2. If you have children who are in junior high school, to what extent have you discussed with them your expectations for their college education? To what extent have you discussed your expectations with your spouse? Again, work with your fiduciary advisor to determine what you can afford. Then discuss your expectations with your children, and reinforce them as needed until they are about to graduate from high school.
3. What are your children's passions? What brings them the most joy? Encourage them to choose a career and life path that contributes to their joy.
4. When your children are exploring their post-secondary education, review the potential return on investment of each program. Consider potential ROI over other factors, such as which college environment appeals most to your children.
5. What did you do today that brought you joy?®

PART 2

Preserving Your Retirement Savings

In Part 2, we focus on *preserving* your retirement savings. Having a personal financial plan prepared by your fiduciary financial advisor and a team of additional experts is critical to having a confident, joy-filled retirement.

Part 2 covers the following four chapters:

Protecting Your Assets and Income

Another important component to planning your financial future is protecting your assets and future income with insurance.

Insurance coverage is really an incredible tool. Simply by getting appropriate and sufficient insurance in place and paying the premiums on time, you transfer the risk of injury, illness, premature death, and loss of assets from yourself to an insurance company.

We build your personal financial plan according to the assets and income you have now and what you want your life to be like in the future, in retirement. If something happened to jeopardize your assets and income, it could derail all your plans and goals— without insurance. But with insurance, you will receive the money you need to maintain your current lifestyle, despite the emergency.

As with all other areas of financial planning, I strongly recommend that you work with your fiduciary advisor to secure the types and amounts of insurance that are right for you and your family.

Protect Everything That Is Valuable to You

By law in most states, we are all required to carry property and casualty (P&C) insurance to cover damage to, or loss of, our vehicles and homes.

Although we are not required by law to carry other important types of insurance, they are incredibly important. In fact, we could argue that life, disability, and long-term care insurance are even more important to your financial future than home and auto insurance because these types of coverage protect losses of typically much larger amounts of money. We'll discuss these types of protection in the next section.

Having insurance coverage in place can make the difference between thriving and going bankrupt in the face of a disaster. Life insurance will ensure that your beneficiaries receive a benefit check if you were to die unexpectedly. Disability insurance will replace your income should you become disabled. Long-term care insurance will provide you with money to obtain in-home care or care in a facility if you become unable to care for yourself.

Those are the most common types of insurance. There are many types of unusual insurance, too. People insure whatever is valuable to them.

For example, supermodel Heidi Klum insured her legs for $2.2 million. Welsh singer Tom Jones insured his chest hair for $7.7 million. Plenty of athletes have insured their body parts.[32]

As we build personal financial plans for the families we work with, protection is a major component. We want to make sure you have adequate coverage for anything you value that would cause a hardship if something happened to that asset—whether it's your income, property, art, collectibles, or something more unusual.

I have a rider on my P&C policy for an original LeRoy Neiman painting in my house. Neiman was an American artist who was known for his brilliantly colored expressionist paintings and screen prints of musicians, athletes, and sporting events. Years ago, we hung the painting on the wall—very securely, we thought. But one day, the painting suddenly came crashing down off the wall. Thankfully, the painting itself didn't incur much damage, but the frame was pretty busted up.

Because I had a rider to protect the loss of that painting, my insurance company paid to restore the painting and the frame back to the condition they were in before they flew off the wall.

---

32. "The 15 Most Bizarre Insurance Policies Ever Written," Morgan O'Rourke, Risk Management Monitor, March 25, 2010, https://www.riskmanagementmonitor.com/the-15-most-bizarre-insurance-policies-ever-written/.

The Big Three: Life, Disability, and Long-Term Care Insurance

For as long as insurance has been around, agents and advisors have faced the challenge of selling protection products to people who do not want to think about, much less discuss, potentially becoming disabled or passing away unexpectedly. Yet these scenarios occur every day.

Failing to plan ahead poses significant risks to your family's financial well-being. Preparing for "What if?" scenarios is always a good idea. For example, make sure your will is up-to-date and that the beneficiaries listed on it match the beneficiaries on your other documents.

We address all these concerns when working with families. Although we do not sell P&C insurance, we ask the families we serve to provide us with their automobile and home P&C insurance decks, and we have strategic partners review them to make sure the coverage is sufficient. Then we focus on ensuring the families we serve are not overlooking the most critical types of insurance: life, disability, and long-term care.

We focus on ensuring the families we serve are not overlooking the most critical types of insurance: life, disability, and long-term care.

The life insurance conversation is really about determining the amount of money your family will need to reach their financial goals if you or your spouse were to pass away unexpectedly.

The disability coverage conversation is more or less, "How will I replace my future income if I become disabled?"

And long-term care is really looking at the pros and cons of self-insuring—using your own assets—in case you or a family member needs long-term care, versus obtaining a policy that will cover those expenses.

Let's take a closer look at these critical types of protection.

Life Insurance

Everyone is aware that they won't live forever, yet most people don't want to talk about this reality. We must have this tough conversation to get life insurance in place, though. Getting properly insured is the most thoughtful, loving gift you can give your family members.

The types of life insurance vary. You can even use some life insurance policies to accrue cash value. What's right for someone else's family probably won't be appropriate for yours. We won't discuss all those nuances here, though; there are plenty of books out there on the details related to life insurance. Here are the two main messages I want to emphasize here:

1. Most people are underinsured.
2. It is critical for you to work with a fiduciary financial advisor to get the right coverage in place.

We are fortunate that, in this country, we can simply purchase insurance coverage to protect our families against these financially devastating situations.

Disability Insurance

People seem to know a little more about life insurance than they do about disability and long-term care insurance. The dollar amounts of these policies often cost significantly more than life insurance in terms of cost per thousand.

But God forbid you become disabled in your forties and can't earn an income. Social Security disability probably isn't going to provide you with enough money for your family to maintain their current lifestyle. A disability policy will enable you and your family to maintain your current lifestyle if someone in the family should become disabled.

Most people don't feel like they will ever become disabled and put in a position where they can't work, but it happens more often than people realize.

People are living longer than ever before, with the exception of the years we have been affected by the

COVID-19 pandemic. Plus, as we make advances in treating debilitating diseases, many of the health issues that used to *kill* us now *disable* us.

In the past twenty years, deaths caused by cancer, heart attack, and stroke have decreased significantly, but *disabilities* caused by those same three conditions have increased dramatically. For example, the number of *deaths* due to hypertension have decreased by 73 percent, but *disabilities* due to hypertension have risen 70 percent.[33]

Many of the health issues that used to *kill* us now *disable* us.

During the course of your career, you are three and a half times more likely to be injured and need disability coverage than you are to die and need life insurance. At no age is the risk of death greater than the risk of becoming disabled.[34]

Although disability is often thought to be an affliction of the older population, it strikes young people more than people realize.

In 2021, it was estimated that one-quarter (25 percent) of 20-year-olds would be out of work for at least a year because of a disability. Also, almost 90

33. "95+ Disability Insurance Stats & Disability Facts (2021)," Aten-Re El, Simply Insurance, February 10, 2022, https://www. simplyinsurance.com/disability-statistics/.
34. "Death vs. Disability," Affordable Insurance Protection.com, date unknown, https://www.affordableinsuranceprotection.com/ death_vs_disability.

percent of long-term disability claims are caused by illnesses, not accidents, and they are not work-related. In fact, 25 percent of short-term disability claims are related to pregnancy.[35]

Those numbers are pretty powerful. If you become disabled at an early age, it will likely inhibit your ability to work, and that's going to impact you and your family significantly. But again, you can easily protect yourself against the hardship related to disability, simply by getting the necessary insurance in place, in sufficient amounts.

Long-Term Care Insurance

Closely related to disability insurance is long-term care insurance. Because we are now living longer than our ancestors did, there is a higher likelihood that some point in the future, many of us will get to the point where we can no longer take care of ourselves. Luckily, long-term care insurance is an incredible solution that can provide you with funds needed to get assistance at home or in a facility, if this should happen.

Many people think long-term care pays benefits only when someone is placed in a nursing home. People say, "I'm never going to a nursing home. I'll figure a way out other than that, but I'm *not* going to a facility." I share that sentiment, and most people do. No one wants

---

35. Ibid.

to end up in a nursing home.

The great news is that long-term care insurance provides for at-home care as well. So if you are no longer able to take care of yourself, you don't have to go to a facility. If you have long-term care insurance in place before that time comes, your coverage will cover the cost of having a caregiver go to your home to provide assistance in your daily routine. Some policies will even pay a family member to provide that care.

> **Long-term care insurance provides for at-home care as well.**

Get Coverage, Regardless of Your Level of Wealth

A family we work with has significant assets. We have worked with them to make sure they have the right P&C, life insurance, and disability coverage. Over the past couple of years, we have begun having conversations about long-term care. Although these are difficult conversations, they are necessary.

It's a bit of a struggle to think about yourself deteriorating in that way, but unless you have enough assets that you can afford long-term care on your own, it's something to think about. Even if you do have enough assets, wouldn't you rather pass that money along to your heirs or to charities you care about than to spend it on caregiving?

We have worked with wealthy families who have decided not to purchase long-term care insurance. They say, "We're willing to take that risk. If a long-term-care need eats into our kids' inheritances, we're fine with that."

That is their choice. They are making that decision with their eyes wide open, and they understand what the risks are. They also understand the upsides of purchasing the insurance but choose not to do so.

What's more common, though, is that people are unaware of their risks and unaware of how insurance products can protect them. Also common is people who are aware of the risks but won't take the time to evaluate the financial impact those risks could have on their families. They don't want to think about it. As a result, they don't investigate the pros and cons, and they don't make an educated decision about whether or not the cost of the insurance is worth what they would pay in premiums.

You can't just fly blind on these things. Yes, it's difficult to accept that life often doesn't go as planned. But as you can see, being properly insured can make the difference between your family having a comfortable lifestyle or having to downgrade your lifestyle in the event of an emergency.

Recently, we were talking with a couple who has two children, ages five and seven. They own an $800,000 home and collectively, they have about $1.5 million worth of coverage on the family.

One and a half million dollars' worth of coverage sounds like a lot of money, right?

They felt confident that it was sufficient to replace any losses that could result from an emergency. But it doesn't seem like a lot when you start factoring in the amount of money it would take to replace their income if one of them passed away.

I asked them, "If one or both of you were to pass away unexpectedly, what would your financial priorities be?"

They said they would want to pay off the mortgage that was still remaining on their $800,000 home to get rid of that debt. They also said they wanted to have money set aside for their two children to get a college education. That's another $300,000. Taking care of just two important expenses has already accounted for close to $1 million of the death benefit they would receive on that $1.5 million policy if one of them were to pass away. It's eaten up already, and we haven't even talked about income replacement for a period of time yet.

A lot of people pick a number arbitrarily and say, "This is a good number. This will be enough coverage; I'm comfortable with it." But most people significantly underestimate the amount of money they will need to cover important expenses. Again, a fiduciary advisor provides priceless value in this area.

To figure out how much life insurance you will need, we reverse-engineer the numbers.

Again, we approach this conversation with people by asking them, "If one or both of you pass away, what would you want to have covered? Do you have debts you would want to pay off? What will your children need? What will your surviving spouse need in terms of funds for the future?"

Then we do the mathematical equation for planning and back into an estimate of how much insurance they need to reach the goals they have stated and to keep their financial plan in place.

The families we serve who have life insurance in place and receive a death-benefit check when a family member dies always express their gratitude for that coverage. Of course that money does not mitigate the grief they experience over the loss of their loved ones, but it certainly makes the transition process a lot easier. Those who have insurance in place are able to focus on their grief and one another instead of worrying about money issues.

The Minimum Required Coverage Usually Isn't Enough

Most people insure their homes and cars according to the minimum required by law in their state. But in most cases, this isn't enough coverage. Beyond obtaining the legal minimum, the P&C conversation is typically, "What's my risk, and how do I cover that?"

Get Coverage While You Are Insurable and Healthy

In general, the earlier you apply for insurance, the better. Apply when you are still insurable, before you are diagnosed with any health conditions that could make you ineligible for the coverage or that could cause you to pay higher premiums.

However, most people do not need to purchase all these types of insurance at one time. For instance, you probably don't need long-term care insurance when you're 30 years old because the risk of needing long-term care at that early age is low for most people. Still, it should be on your radar.

I do encourage you to get life and disability insurance in place as early as possible, though. There are a few reasons for this.

One is that your needs for coverage will change over time. The life insurance you take out on yourself when you're 25 years old, still single, and not yet a homeowner will be much different from the life insurance you'll need when you are 40 years old, are married with several children, and have a mortgage and other valuable assets. Also, your income will likely be higher at age 40 than at age 25, so you will need coverage to protect that higher amount of income.

A second reason to obtain coverage early is that you are more likely to be insurable when you are younger, before any medical diagnoses pop up that could render you uninsurable or a greater risk. Your premiums will be lower if you get insurance in place while your health is excellent.

Like your overall financial plan, your insurance coverage needs to be reevaluated over time because of your changing needs over time.

You are more likely to be insurable when you are younger.

Your fiduciary advisor will constantly ensure that your coverage is appropriate for your needs. This often means making sure your policies slide higher to adjust as your income increases and adding new coverage as necessary over time.

The earlier you get insurance coverage, the better off you will be in terms of rates and opportunities. You are most likely in better health right now than you will ever be, so you can most likely get your least-expensive policy today. Don't wait!

My goal is to show families that they need to address these important topics. Each family will tackle them differently in terms of the types of policies they buy and the amounts of coverage they obtain. But as long as we're discussing protection, they are beginning to understand their potential risks if they do not get coverage and their potential benefits if they do get coverage in place.

Except for the ultra-well-off, who are in a different stratosphere in terms of wealth, most people cannot afford to risk facing the future without insurance protection. They start adding it all up—"Well, I need to put money in my 401(k) retirement plan, pay off my mortgage, save for our kids' college education, and plan for retirement." Typically, there comes a point where there's just not enough juice in the orange to fill all these buckets.

Insurance coverage ensures that your orange has ample juice for now and the future!

We Are Like Switzerland

As you seek out a fiduciary advisor, please note what type of organization the advisor is affiliated with. I believe you will receive the best options if you work with an independent advisor—one who is not "captive" to a certain company or compensated in a way that encourages him or her to focus on one financial service over the other.

For example, if you go to traditional insurance-based agents or advisors, they're probably going to lead with life insurance, or insurance in general, because that's their bread and butter. That's what their company specializes in, and it's what they know. On the other hand, advisors who work for large brokerage firms are probably going to lead with investments. Their focus will be on building your portfolio of investments in an effort to optimize your return. That's their bread and butter and what they do best.

At Mitlin, we're an island. We're like Switzerland—neutral. When we work with families, we look at everything equally—whatever is best for that family. We want to address their situation, their concerns, their biggest risks, and their goals for the future. In just about every case, that involves an appropriate focus on protection, investments, and personal financial planning. It also involves each client's level of risk tolerance and what worries them most.

One family might worry that one of the income earners might pass away unexpectedly. Another family's biggest concern may be having enough money for retirement. And another family's biggest concern may be an elderly relative's health decline.

Some families have just a couple of concerns; others have many concerns, with varying levels of worry and risk associated with them. We will start our discussions and planning based on what is of greatest concern to them. Because we have no "master to serve," we do whatever makes the most sense to get the families we serve on the path they need to be on to protect their legacy.

This is the essence of the way we approach personal financial planning. For all the families we serve, we address their concerns, their risks, their gaps in protection, and their hopes and dreams for the future. Getting these areas taken care of increases their confidence and enables them to derive the most joy possible from their lives.

Types of Insurance Coverage That Are Necessary but Often Overlooked

The following are additional areas of protection that many people need but often overlook.

1. Umbrella Insurance

Under the umbrella of necessary coverage is an umbrella policy—no pun intended. Umbrella insurance provides additional liability coverage beyond the amounts of liability insurance you already have in your auto and homeowner policies. It covers all sorts of situations—for example, if your dog bites someone, if you or your child causes damage to someone's home, if someone hurts themselves on your property, or if someone sues you for libel or slander.

What we've found is that most people are underinsured. Yet umbrella coverage is much more affordable than people realize, and it's easy to increase your protection.

Umbrella coverage is much more affordable than people realize.

2. Uninsured/Underinsured Motorist Coverage

In many cases, the auto insurance policies people have are inadequate to protect their financial responsibility in the case of an accident that's deemed to be their fault.

Let's say you cause an auto accident that injures a family of four, and your insurance policy covers liability up to $500,000. That sounds like a lot of money, but it won't be nearly enough coverage if that family sues you for $2 million to cover their medical bills and vehicle repair or replacement.

Here in New York and in other states, some insurance companies sell insurance riders to protect drivers against the potential costs of accidents involving uninsured or underinsured motorists. If a motorist with no insurance hit your vehicle, there would be no insurance company to pay for your car repairs and medical bills. You can cover that potential risk simply by getting this particular rider on your policy.

In states that have a higher percentage of uninsured and/or underinsured motorists, the premiums can be a little higher, but the need for this coverage is more likely to be needed.

3. Life Insurance on Stay-at-Home Parents

When people think about protecting their family's financial future, they often focus on insuring just the primary income earner's income. Typically, they buy life insurance that would be sufficient to cover the family's financial future if something were to happen to that person.

The spouse who doesn't work outside the home often gets overlooked in the insurance component. We see a lot of people falling short in this area, and we make sure to cover the risk of losing that person as well. If something were to happen to that spouse, the family would likely face hardship, just as if something happened to the primary income earner. The surviving spouse would need to replace child care and transport, food shopping and preparation, yard care, and other important activities at home.

Years ago, I was chatting with my cousin, whose wife was a stay-at-home mom, and the subject of life insurance came up. He said to me, "Larry, she earns no money. Why would she need life insurance?"

My response outlined all the tasks he would have to pay someone to do if she were no longer around to do them. He hadn't thought about it like that before.

Several organizations have attempted to put a dollar value on the value of a stay-at-home parent. Insure.com figures the wage a mom should earn for the 18 or so jobs she must tackle throughout the day was $126,725 in 2022, which is 9.2 percent higher than the previous year's estimate of $116,022. Salary.com's Annual Mom Salary Survey from May 2021 calculated that moms should be paid a lot more than that: $184,820.[36]

So if you are the primary income earner and you and your spouse have two children, you will still earn your income if your spouse dies. But who's going to take care of the kids in the same fashion your spouse has done? It will be difficult to find someone else who could provide the care that even comes close to the level of the other parent. You need life insurance coverage on the nonworking spouse so you will have a pool of money to use for child care and other priorities if something were to happen to that spouse.

4. Trusts

I've mentioned that we consult with strategic partners on certain financial situations, one of which is trusts. Trusts can protect your assets from creditors, predators, and legal issues upon your death.

A *trust* is a fiduciary arrangement that allows a third party, or trustee, to hold assets on behalf of beneficiaries. Trusts allow you to maintain control over your assets upon your death because you are specifying, in advance, exactly how and when the

Trusts can protect your assets from creditors, predators, and legal issues upon your death.

---

36. "Here's How Much Economists Say Stay-at-Home Moms Should Get Paid," Cameron Huddleston, GOBankingRates, May 25, 2022, https://www.gobankingrates.com/money/jobs/how-much-stay-at-home-moms-should-make/.

assets will pass to your beneficiaries. Trusts also prevent your surviving family members from the inconvenience and delays related to probate, a process they would have to go through if you did not specify how you wanted your assets to be handled upon your death.

Plus, if you arrange for an irrevocable trust, it may not be considered part of your taxable estate, so fewer taxes may be due upon your death. Assets in a trust also may be able to pass outside of probate, which saves family members time, hassles, and court fees. A trust can potentially reduce estate taxes as well.

Be sure to speak with your fiduciary advisor about a trust so you can rest assured that your assets will be handled according to your wishes.

Planning for the future does not mean you are a pessimist, expecting the worst. It simply means you care about your family enough to secure protection against all kinds of risks. Looking out into the future, our human tendency is that we want to think of things in the best possible light. But the reality is, unfortunate things happen. Every day, people's assets are encumbered or potentially encumbered because of a risk to their financial future because of death, disability, or a family member needing long-term care.

The solution is simple—work with your fiduciary

advisor to assess what types and amounts of coverage you need, and get it in place—sooner rather than later. Being protected against risks can replace any worry you have experienced in your life with the capacity to increase your joy.

In the next chapter—as promised—we'll look at the important social and mental aspects of retirement.

Chapter 7—Making It Personal

1. What is important to you and would create a loss for you if something were to happen to that asset? Work with your fiduciary advisor to get insurance protection in place to protect its loss. It doesn't matter how unusual it is—if it's valuable to you, insure it!

2. To what extent do you have sufficient life insurance coverage on you *and* your spouse? If you have none, or not enough, please make it a priority to secure this coverage as soon as possible. Keep in mind that most people are underinsured and that stay-at-home parents are often overlooked.

3. If you are in your fifties or sixties, please speak with your fiduciary advisor about getting long-

term care insurance in place.

4. If you do not have an umbrella policy in place to protect you and your family against losses including lawsuits, please get one in place. This type of coverage is extremely affordable.

5. What did you today that brought you joy?*

How to Plan for Retirement– Mentally and Socially

I believe there is a misconception—an underestimation—of our role as financial advisors. Our title puts the focus on the "financial" aspect of planning, yet competent, thorough financial advisors guide you in ancillary areas as well. At Mitlin, we consider *all* aspects of your life when building your personal financial plan—financially, mentally, and socially.

Awareness Leads to Planning and Then to Fulfillment

The first step in addressing a more all-encompassing view of retirement is to be aware of the various aspects. I want to open people's eyes to the fact that the mental and social components of retirement are also important as we develop their plan together. Plenty of people have estimated the amount of money they will need in retirement accurately, yet they are unhappy in retirement because they failed to address these other critical components of life.

For example, when we ask what people's hobbies are, sometimes they say, "I don't have any. I never had time for hobbies." We want them to enter retirement with some meaningful activities already a part of their lives, so we encourage them to start exploring some activities that seem fun to them now and not wait until they retire.

Just as you can't expect to save a million dollars if you begin saving just a few years before retirement, you can't expect to build a strong mental and social framework for

> **We want them to enter retirement with some meaningful activities already a part of their lives.**

retirement if you wait until you're about to retire. I encourage you to begin thinking about these concepts and working on them now. A little planning now will put you in the best position for when you do retire.

Preparation is a key ingredient of a successful retirement.

A 2022 study from The Harris Poll and Edward Jones shows that the people who take more steps to prepare for their retirement journey tend to enjoy their retirement the most. Retirees who report having a high quality of life in retirement reported that they began saving earlier on average and were less likely to make early withdrawals from retirement accounts than those retirees with a lower quality of life. They were also more likely to take care of their health before retirement; discuss retirement goals with family and friends;

and explore new pastimes, hobbies, and interests to help boost their sense of purpose in retirement. The retirees who were enjoying the highest quality of life in retirement said their top three smartest financial actions to prepare for retirement were starting to save early (and consistently), maximizing contributions, and working with a financial advisor. [37]

Because people have been taught to think about the money aspect of retirement, most haven't thought through the other aspects. We tend to get inquisitive stares from people who are planning to retire when we ask them, "What are you planning to do with that free time?"

In a lot of cases, people are just burned out from working and need to slow down and take a rest. That is certainly understandable, but we encourage them to engage in meaningful activities at some point. Very early in the retirement-planning process, we try to educate people about the importance of planning how they will spend their free time, how their relationships could change, where they plan to live once they retire, and other aspects of the infrastructure they've built up over their lives that could change.

For example, if they're moving from New York to Florida and they've never spent time in Florida, do they

37. "Longevity and the New Journey to Retirement," Edward Jones, June 2022, https://www.edwardjones.com/sites/default/files/ac-quiadam/2022-07/AW_EJ_NewJourneyExecSummary.pdf.

have enough interests and people down there to keep them busy while they're not working anymore?

All the Elements Are Connected

As we start having deeper conversations with the families we serve about what they want retirement to look like, that's when we begin exploring the nonfinancial aspects. The discussion about money is actually a great segue for us to ask, "How do you plan to spend those forty or fifty hours per week that you were spending at work?" Then we can discuss how the families we serve will navigate the other aspects of retirement.

One day recently, I had conversations with two different people, before 1:00 p.m., about the mental and social impacts of retirement.

One of those conversations was with a gentleman who owns a second-generation family business. He is 64 years old and wants to retire in five years or so.

I told him, "Jim, if you retire in five years, you will still be relatively young. What will life look like for you when you retire? Do you want to continue working at least part-time?"

Jim said, "You know, now that I think about it, I guess you could say I'm already retired to some degree. I work when I want to, and if I want to go away or on vacation, I do so. I have structured my work in a way that enables me to have that freedom."

As we discussed his future more, Jim added, "But if I do fully retire, I don't know what I'm going to do with all the free time."

Unlike many people, Jim is working because he wants to—not because he has to, financially speaking. So, even though he is making a gradual transition to full retirement, he isn't sure how to ensure the mental and social aspects of his life in retirement are fulfilling for him.

The second conversation I had recently about the mental and social aspects of retirement was with a woman named Stephanie. We were already working with her husband, Stewart.

Stephanie shared with me that Stewart was thinking about retiring in the next few years, partly because his long commute to and from work—about an hour each way—was beginning to wear him down. Despite the post-pandemic work-from-home boom, Stewart's company would not allow him to work from home or remotely. However, he wasn't sure he wanted to retire completely. He thought he might want to work in some sort of part-time job, closer to home, because he didn't know how he would fill all that free time. We worked with both of them to get a clearer picture of what their lives would be like, given several "What if?" scenarios.

We include all your priorities in life, represented by the spokes of the wheel, in your personal financial plan. That means we have to include them in your budget as well.

It's not our job to tell you what to do; it's our job to help you prepare for a smoother transition to your next stage of life, whatever that is going to be. And then we serve as a sounding board and accountability partner on your journey, monitoring and adjusting your personal plan as needed along the way.

The Mental Aspects of Retiring

Many people, eager to step out of the workforce, jump into retirement head-first once they believe they have enough money to retire. But most do nothing to prepare themselves for the change *mentally*. You won't know what it's like to have complete freedom from work until you have reached that point—but preparation can help ensure it's a positive transition.

What we often see is that those first few weeks of freedom from work are often blissful—but then the freedom can become overwhelmingly empty. It's not the work itself that's missing; it's the sense of *purpose*. It's the joy. There comes a point for most people when waking up each morning without having anything to strive for becomes stressful. We don't want to see this happen! Retirement should ease your stress, not add to it, and this is the outcome you can look forward to with proper planning.

> **Those first few weeks of freedom from work are often blissful—but then the freedom can become overwhelmingly empty.**

Research isn't clear about whether retirement tends to improve or diminish people's well-being. For every article that claims retiring can *benefit* our mental and physical health, there's another article claiming that retiring leads to *diminished* mental and physical health. This is because everyone will experience retirement differently, based on many different factors. I believe those who plan every aspect of their retirement—financial, mental, and social—in advance have a much better chance of thriving in retirement.

Some research indicates that retirement is the happiest time in life—for people who are prepared. Research from Age Wave and Merrill Lynch found that, of all periods in life, people are happiest and most content between the ages of 65 and 74. While 76 percent of people in this age range said they "often feel happy," only 51 percent of 25- to 34-year-olds said the same. Similar numbers were reported for people who said they "often feel content" and "often feel relaxed." The younger group experienced more anxiety, with 37 percent of them saying they "often feel anxiety," while only 12 percent of the 65- to 74-year-olds often felt anxious.[38]

On the flip side of that discussion, other researchers have found that retirement can lead to undesirable

---

38. "Most People Find That Retirement Is the Happiest Period of Life," Kathleen Coxwell, MoneyTalksNews, November 9, 2021, https://www.moneytalksnews.com/slideshows/life-after-retirement-is-going-to-be-great-if-you-are-truly-ready/.

emotions—especially for those who did not prepare. Some researchers estimate that almost one-third of retirees in the United States develop symptoms of depression when they retire. Others experience anxiety. Anger is another common emotion some retirees experience—especially if they were forced out of the workforce.[39]

Relationship issues can surface as well, as couples who spent little time together during their working years are suddenly face-to-face every day, all day. For this reason, it is important that you include your spouse in all aspects of your retirement planning so you can both prepare for this major life transition. Even if—*especially* if—this is a difficult conversation to have, it needs to be addressed. Your financial advisor can help you start the discussion with your spouse.

Now let's take a closer look at the *social* aspects of retiring.

The Social Aspects of Retiring

Some of our most enduring friendships emerge from the workplace, as we share a common work environment and experiences with our colleagues. Of course those friendships can continue once people

---

39. "Retirement Depression: Coping with the Emotional Pain," PsychCentral, May 13, 2022, https://psychcentral.com/depression/retirement-depression.

retire, but sometimes that just doesn't happen. It's important to replace that social structure with a new one.

You probably don't plan to sit in front of the TV for 40 hours a week once you're no longer working. So, how *will* you spend your time, and with whom? I encourage you to put a new infrastructure in place before you retire—relationships and activities. In advance, figure out how you will replace your time at work with other meaningful endeavors—and with whom.

Put a new infrastructure in place before you retire—relationships and activities. As mentioned, it's surprising how many people we encounter who have no hobbies because they never had the time for them. I strongly recommend developing some hobbies before you retire. Explore a wide variety of activities to discover what you enjoy most. Don't wait until you're retired!

Can you guess what most retirees want to devote their time to once they retire? The Harris Poll I just mentioned found that 65 percent of survey respondents wanted to spend more quality time with family and friends. Coming in as a close second, 59 percent said they wanted to take steps to improve their health. Another 43 percent wanted to travel/take vacations, and 32 percent wanted to engage in creative projects or hobbies. Only 10 percent said work was their top priority.[40]

Many of the families we serve who are retired or planning to retire express an interest in charitable inclinations, while some want to travel. Others want to be more active; I know a lot of older folks who are taking up pickleball.

Social interaction might seem inconsequential in the larger picture, but it is actually tied to our sense of purpose.

A study published in the July 2022 issue of the *American Journal of Geriatric Psychiatry* found that having positive social interactions is associated with older adults' sense of purposefulness, which can fluctuate from day to day. These interactions are more strongly correlated to purposefulness in people who are retired. The researchers discovered that the more positive interactions a person had during the day, the more purposeful they reported feeling in the evening. Other measures, including employment and relationship status, did *not* predict a person's sense of purpose.[41]

For this study, the research team defined having a sense of purpose as "the extent to which people feel they have personally meaningful goals and directions

---

40. "Longevity and the New Journey to Retirement," Edward Jones, June 2022, https://www.edwardjones.com/sites/default/files/acquiadam/2022-07/AW_EJ_NewJourneyExecSummary.pdf.
41. "Social Interactions Tied to Sense of Purpose," Brandie Jefferson, Washington University in St. Louis, July 6, 2022, https://source.wustl.edu/2022/07/social-interactions-tied-to-sense-of-purpose/.

guiding them through life." Having a sense of purpose is about more than feeling good. Prior research has shown that adults with a higher sense of purpose lead longer, healthier, and happier lives. They have lower rates of Alzheimer's disease and of heart and other cardiovascular problems.[42]

A 2021 study by Kiplinger found seven characteristics common among people who are happy in retirement. Two of those are that the happy retirees find a clear sense of purpose, and they foster strong social connections.[43]

So that sense of purpose I mentioned in chapter 1, "Find Your *Why*," isn't only a component of our careers. It's closely woven into our personal interactions as well. For this reason, we need to be mindful about surrounding ourselves with people who support and encourage us and who have similar interests. We need to ask ourselves why we choose to spend time with the people around us. In some cases, this self-analysis can reveal that we need to rethink some of our social relationships.

---

42. Ibid.
43. "Happy Retirees Have These 7 Habits in Common," Jacob Schroeder, Kiplinger, June 30, 2021, https://www.kiplinger.com/ retirement/happy-retirement/601160/7-surprisingly-valuable-as-sets-for-a-happy-retirement.

Expect the Best, but Plan for the Worst

From a financial standpoint, again, we err on the conservative side and plan for the worst-case scenario— just to be safe. For example, someone might want to retire at age 67, but then health issues arise that force him or her to retire at age 62. With proper planning, unexpected circumstances like that are much easier for you to manage. Again, we explore many different "What if?" scenarios with the families we serve to cover all possible bases.

I always say it's best to plan for the worst and hope for the best. If you plan for the worst but your situation works out for the best, you will be in a great position. But if the opposite happens, you want to have a plan in place for adjusting in light of the new circumstances. Planning ahead and being prepared can minimize the disruption to your life when the unexpected arises.

A couple we work with was approaching retirement and planning for that transition. She wanted to retire fully, while her husband loved working and liked being out and about, but he didn't want to work as often or as much as he had. So he was going to work part-time. Three months before they were due to retire, the husband had a stroke. Talk about a change of plans! Their original plan might not come to fruition now that he has suffered a stroke. He might not be able to work again at all.

This is just one example of unforeseen, unexpected situations that can arise. They can derail your plans without proper planning. This is why we like to err on the conservative side and plan for the worst.

Some People Will Never Retire

Sometimes, we meet people whom we suspect will never retire, based on their personalities and the strong link between their work and their identity. Even if they talk about retirement, we doubt that they will ever actually do it. And that's OK.

Certain people probably *should* never retire. Work is the only way they can fulfill their ongoing need for stimulation and a sense of accomplishment. Maybe at some point, they'll slow down. They won't go 100 miles an hour like they did their entire careers, but they will still stay actively involved in their work.

I will know I'm ready to retire when I wake up one day and know that I don't necessarily *have* to go to work. I'm not sure I will ever quit working entirely because I really enjoy what I do. And that's another mental component of retirement. If I really enjoy what I do, is it really work? Not really. It's something I enjoy, and it's part of my life.

"The Great Resignation" Was Really "The Great Exploration"

During the COVID-19 pandemic, we heard a lot about "The Great Resignation"—the unprecedented mass exodus of Americans from the US workforce. Between January 2021 and February 2022 alone, nearly 57 million Americans quit their jobs.[44]

In a *Harvard Business Review* article, Mike Clementi, executive vice president of human resources at Unilever, calls this shift "The Great Exploration." He says that moniker better addresses the underlying cause rather than the mass exodus itself. "Pandemic life forced everyone to reexamine their personal and professional priorities," Clementi writes. "Remote work alerted us to the possibility of decoupling jobs from geography. And a seller's labor market empowers us to pursue it. It's a personal awakening incubating an exploratory movement that is reshaping how and why we work, live, and think about our futures."

I agree that the pandemic was an eye-opener for a lot of people—a personal awakening. They began to realize that their employers hadn't been very flexible in the past. And then they began to wonder why. Others

44. "The Great Resignation Stems from a Great Exploration," Keith Ferrazzi and Mike Clementi, *Harvard Business Review*, June 22, 2022, https://hbr.org/2022/06/the-great-resignation-stems-from-a-great-exploration.

began to realize that they had been putting in a lot of effort and not receiving much acknowledgment of their contributions—or appropriate compensation. Still others realized they were deriving no joy from their work. So they began to seek out better opportunities. In the process, many of them became happier, healthier, and more fulfilled.

This means that, for many, the pandemic didn't *cause* people to resign from their jobs *en masse*; it simply prompted them to reconsider what they were doing with their lives and to pivot to something more fulfilling.

Recently, we had a conversation with a woman we serve who is in her mid-forties. She has been thinking about taking on a new role because her company went back to a hybrid work schedule—some days in the office and some days working remotely. She prefers to work 100 percent remotely. She said, "I don't want my employer telling me when I have to work, when I should be in the office, when I should be doing this or that. It's much more convenient for me if I put in my forty hours a week when it works for me. What does it matter if I do it nine-to-five or a few hours here and a few there?"

> **For many, the pandemic simply prompted them to reconsider what they were doing with their lives and to pivot to something more fulfilling**

To me, this is a refreshing and welcome awakening—a much-needed infusion of awareness about what's really important to us in life. We need to apply this awareness to our current careers as well as to retirement.

The trend toward remote work gives people opportunities to work longer in their careers. Added flexibility, and freedom from a commute to an office, may enable more people to work longer than they had anticipated—if they want to. It all depends on what each individual wants and needs.

I encourage you to assess your career now and determine if you need to make any changes. That self-assessment process will also lead you closer to a retirement that enables you to live your best life possible.

Consider a Gradual Exit from the Workforce

It can be quite an abrupt transition—working full-time for decades and then, all of a sudden, not working at all. Many retirees find that a *gradual* exit from the workforce makes it easier to adjust financially, mentally, and socially.

Part-time work can serve as a bridge between your career and retirement. It can ease the often jarring impact of that transition. Some people make arrangements with their current employers to scale down from full-time to part-time work. Others engage in consulting work a few years before retirement to see if that might be an enjoyable way to step down from a full-time career. And for others, retirement offers a chance to work part-time in a field that's entirely different from the work they did in their full-time careers.

Whatever option works best for you, part-time work gives you a chance to test-drive a slower pace of life instead of just hitting a certain age and then slamming on the brakes altogether. Part-time work enables you to continue seeking out mental challenges and to continue nurturing friendships—or building new ones.

From there, you can start creating an environment that allows you to fill up your free time once you do retire. You might enjoy your part-time work so much that you continue it once you retire. Or maybe you will find that you're enjoying the things you're doing in your free time, and the relationships you've built around your hobbies, more than you enjoy your part-time work.

Having this bridge from full-time work to retirement enables you to explore your options. You don't have to work part-time in perpetuity. Just use it to build the infrastructure you want to have in place once you retire and to discover what gives you the most joy and fulfillment.

Begin Where You Are

As I mentioned earlier, most of the families we serve at Mitlin come to us well before retirement is even on the horizon for them. Yet most of them do not come to us for retirement planning initially. Typically, people come to us because they have a number of accounts in different places, and they don't have a point person who is advising them on their overall situation. They are seeking out an overarching game plan and somebody who will take a leadership role to help them put their personal financial plan together and lead them through the plan.

A lot of people have done a great job of saving money, but when they start to look at retirement, they're not sure where they stand. With assets spread out among several different financial institutions and retirement plans, they don't know how everything is working together toward their end goal. And again, many of them have no idea what their end goal *is*. When they sit down with us, we help crystallize that for them. We help bring a vision to their goals and objectives, combine all their assets into one location, and put a personal financial plan in motion that will optimize their ability to retire confidently.

A woman we've worked with for a while recently began thinking about retiring. She had assets with many different firms, but she had no plan. I asked her, "To what extent do you think you are on track to get where you want to be?"

Her answer was, "I really don't know. I don't even have a track to gauge it on."

We began combining all her assets in one place and discovering her vision, goals, and objectives. We wanted to get a "lay of the land" to see where she was and how we could get her to where she wants to be.

Some of the families we work with are on track, but many are not. That's OK—you have to begin where you are! Once we get that personal financial plan in place, we can adjust it as needed for any circumstance.

Chapter 8—Making It Personal

1. How satisfied are you with your career right now, if you're still working? Is it possible that you, like millions of other Americans, need to consider a different opportunity?

2. What might bring you *mental* fulfillment in retirement? What can you do to begin getting that infrastructure in place now? What might bring you *social* fulfillment in retirement? What can you do to begin getting that in place now?

3. Think about the people you spend time with socially. Do they encourage and support your goals and desired lifestyle? If not, consider making some changes.

4. What hobbies do you have now or have you wished you had time to do? If you don't have any hobbies, begin exploring them now, and then do some "test runs" to see if they align with the lifestyle you plan to have in retirement.

5. What did you do today that brought you joy?®

Taxes Affect Every Financial Decision

The purpose of the personal financial plan we design for you is to help ensure you and your family successfully reach your goals and objectives. The tax considerations that accompany every financial decision are a huge part of that ongoing journey.

Taxes impact the amount of money you actually have at your disposal—net, after tax. This is somewhat of a moving target because your investment values change over time, as do tax rates and ramifications and your goals for the future.

This is one key reason why we must continually review your personal financial plan as a game plan for you and your family. As important factors change, we must review your plan in the context of those new details. It is important for families to look at their decision-making process along the way and determine how taxes might affect their situation.

Again, your situation is unique to you. Not everybody is going to be best served by putting money in a traditional individual retirement account (IRA) or putting all their retirement money into a traditional 401(k). There are definitely some great opportunities with each option, and it makes sense for some folks to use a Roth IRA or a Roth 401(k) option, depending on their circumstances and goals. The difference is that money you withdraw from a Roth version of those accounts is tax-free, whereas the traditional versions of the 401(k) plan and IRA are taxable.

In general, regarding both your retirement accounts and your traditional investments outside retirement, you want to manage those investments in the most tax-efficient way possible.

We want you to keep as much of your money as legally possible. Better tax management equates to more joy in your life!

Many books have been written on the ins and outs of taxes, and those details are beyond the scope of this book. In this chapter, I simply want to make you aware of some key tax-related areas to be aware of as you work with your fiduciary advisor to build your personal financial plan.

Taxes Affect Everyone, Regardless of Financial Status

There are tax implications of every financial decision *anyone* makes, regardless of how much or how little money they have.

Whether you are earning $50,000 or $500,000,

you will have to pay taxes. The only difference is that the tax rate and the tax implications to the person earning $500,000 will be more substantial than the person earning $50,000. The idea is to keep as much of your income as you can, whether it comes from work or investments.

One of our goals in building your personal financial plan is to keep you from paying more tax than you need to. Taxes are an important aspect of every financial plan. We want to manage your tax liability as well as possible so you are not inadvertently giving money to the government that you could use to supplement your lifestyle and save for the future.

> **One of our goals in building your personal financial plan is to keep you from paying more tax than you need to.**

Whatever your situation, we want to put you in the best position to retain as much of your income as possible—today, tomorrow, and in perpetuity.

We Have to Start Where You Are Now

When we assess how taxes will affect your financial situation, a good starting point is to consider which tax bracket you are in for the current year.

Because tax rules and other factors often change, we know that some of the decisions we make about your financial plan today will need to change in the future—but we don't know how just yet. So we begin by considering the tax bracket you are in and tax implications of your situation right now, in the moment.

We have to model the plan on what we know now. Then we make adjustments as the rules and facts change. We have to start somewhere!

For example, if we knew tax rates were going to go up significantly next year, it may make sense for some families to accelerate Roth conversions (more about this later in this chapter). We might find that it is in their best interest for them to accelerate selling certain assets and pay the taxes now versus waiting until later.

We also have to adjust short-term and long-term decisions on each family's personal views. If someone we serve believes tax rates will be significantly higher in the future, then we may have to adjust our planning based on their thoughts. Or if they think tax rates are going to be significantly lower in the future, we may have to adjust our planning based on that belief.

Sometimes, that simply means showing them separate versions of the same plan. The "base case" is what is likely to happen if tax rates stay the same. And then we can explore what might happen if tax rates go up and also if they go down. These scenarios will affect people's short- and long-term decisions. But just like everything else, you have to establish that base case of the plan and then adjust it over time, according to the facts and circumstances at any given point in time.

Timing is critically important when you adjust your investments. For example, if you buy an asset or an investment and hold onto it for ten or eleven months and decide to sell it, we need to look at how the timing will affect your outcome. In some cases, it makes sense to wait and hold off on selling the asset until you hit that twelve-month-and-one-day mark because it's going to shift from a short-term capital gain to a long-term capital gain, which may be taxed at a lower rate and more advantageous.

It's important for us to evaluate how any potential decision will affect you not only today, but in the future as well. This is why it's helpful for us to know if you anticipate being in a higher tax bracket (or lower) in the future. Your tax bracket impacts many decisions you'll make.

Understanding Capital Gains and the Step-Up in Basis

Another tax-related factor we need to look at through the life cycle of a family is capital gains.

If you sell a property, stocks, bonds, or some other type of investment, the difference between the price paid for an asset and the price at which you sold it is either a capital gain or a capital loss. If you sell an asset for *more* than you paid for it, it is considered a *capital gain*. If you sell an asset and receive less than you paid for it, then it is a *capital loss*.

The tax rates for capital gains depend on the amount of time you have owned the investment, the amount of capital gain you have received, and how much your annual income is. Over the years, Congress has made several changes to how capital gains are taxed, from the tax rates themselves to what gets counted as a capital gain.

In one of the families we serve, the matriarch is in her eighties. She has some significant assets in individual securities, and she would love to sell them. They have achieved only marginal growth over the past several years, so she would love to liquidate those assets and transition them somewhere else.

She has accumulated some huge capital gains because she has owned these securities for a very long time. If she were to liquidate them, she would face a potentially large tax liability. Yet if she holds on to the securities and passes away while owning them, then her children will essentially get a step-up in basis under current law, basically eliminating the taxable gains.

A *step-up in basis* applies to investment assets that are passed on after the asset owner's death. It is an IRS tax rule used to adjust the value of an inherited asset to conform to its fair market value for tax purposes. The purpose is to reduce the capital gains tax burden that is assessed on the inherited property.

When we discussed this with her, we showed her what her tax liability would be if we liquidated her securities while she is still living, compared with what it would be if she decided to hold on to them until she passes away. Ideally, we want to ensure that her children incur no tax liability when they inherit these assets. She chose to hold on to the securities because she does not want to pay huge capital gains. With this decision to wait, she is not giving up a lot, but she is probably going to save her family quite a bit in taxes, so it is a wise approach for her.

Many times, people sell assets that they would have been better off holding on to, passing along to the next generation, and using the step-up in basis.

I think this is something that families often overlook. Many times, people sell assets that they would have been better off holding on to, passing along to the next generation, and using the step-up in basis. This often happens because people simply don't know about this tax rule and what it entails. Simply being aware of this rule is a start in the right direction.

Again, I strongly encourage you to work with a fiduciary advisor to explore your options and make wise choices.

Many times, when a loved one passes away and beneficiaries inherit securities, the custodian of those assets does not automatically update the cost basis to the day of death. We have instructed quite a few to do this. If this step gets overlooked, the surviving family members could face a potentially large tax liability that they could have avoided.

This is just one more of many examples showing how important it is that we look at your financial situation, and design your financial plan, through the lens of tax impact. Again, it is a huge part of the financial decision-making process.

We Work Closely with Our Tax Experts

Navigating the tax impacts of your financial decisions is a team effort. Mitlin Financial does not provide tax advice because we are not CPAs. When assisting the families we serve, we regularly consult with their CPAs and with our Advanced Solutions Team, which is made up of CPAs, attorneys, and trust professionals, to determine the best way to manage the tax implications of the financial plans we are designing.

Although we might have the best understanding of a family's *overall* situations, our tax professionals often have the best view of their *tax* situations. It is critical that we assess all "What if?" scenarios and cover all bases because one tax mistake can make a huge difference in your financial situation. Many mistakes are costly and irreversible, so we must get it right.

Together, we build solutions that make sense for you in terms of planning, investments, and taxes and from a holistic standpoint. We make sure you are on board with the strategies we are recommending and understand them fully.

In 2022, when the markets were down, we were able to go into families' non-qualified, non-retirement investment accounts and sell some holdings at a loss—to capture that loss and invest it elsewhere. Then we would wait 31 days and buy those assets back. We help coordinate with our families' accountants to see if the families need losses to offset either other capital gains they have elsewhere or income they have elsewhere. Basically, we go into their portfolios harvest those losses to help lower their tax liability for the year. We work very closely with our team of tax experts and accountants during this process.

One of the couples we work with has built up some significant capital gains in their accounts over the past 10 or 15 years. Their risk profile has changed as they have gotten older, so we're looking to make some changes to the overall strategy for their portfolio.

If we had made those changes right away, this family would have incurred around $300,000 in capital gains. We definitely wanted to avoid that scenario, and there was no reason to change the strategy immediately anyway. We spoke to them about it. We weren't sure if maybe they had some capital loss carryovers or some tax losses that might offset a large portion of these capital gains if we were to take them. So we called the family to ask if they were OK with us having a conversation with their CPA. They said that was fine.

After speaking with the CPA, we devised a plan to unwind the portfolio and shift it over the next 36 months to alleviate the tax liability over a period of time. Making these changes over a three-year period instead of all in one year basically prevented the family from taking a huge tax hit in one year. The CPA agreed that if something changed in the family's tax situation, such as if they experienced some large losses in a subsequent year, we could consider accelerating the shift.

Because we were proactive about having these conversations, we likely saved the family from experiencing a huge tax bill. When we work as a team, we get the benefit of different perspectives, experiences, and skills.

As your family's fiduciary, your wealth advisory team, we always act in your best interest. We believe we can do that more effectively when we are coordinating with other professionals rather than just making decisions in a vacuum by ourselves. We don't want to end up in a situation where we do what we think is right with the information we know, and then at tax time, we get a call from a client who says, "Hey, why did I have this huge capital gain? My accountant is asking why we did this all in one year and why we didn't do it in three?"

Each of us knows our expertise, and we provide the services we are qualified to provide *and* work together to make the best use of everyone's talents. We coordinate with other professionals to make sure we're all on the same page and doing what's best for the families we serve.

A Simple Misunderstanding Could Be Costly

One woman we serve has three grown sisters. Their mom was in failing health, and it looked like she would not live more than a few months. So the four siblings were working with their estate-planning attorney to decide the best strategy for transferring ownership of their mom's assets.

The sister we work with came to us and shared with us her perception of what the estate-planning attorney was planning to do with regard to her mom's estate. It was her understanding that the attorney was planning to gift some of her mom's individual assets to the daughters before she passed.

That didn't sound right to me because doing that would cause the daughter, our client, to lose the step-up in basis that she would have received if her mom simply willed those assets to her, as a beneficiary on the account. Among the four sisters, that step-up in basis would have totaled $100,000 to $150,000 in tax liability.

Before doing anything, I knew I needed to speak with the estate-planning attorney, so I got our client's permission to make that call. I wanted to find out exactly what the attorney was planning to do with those assets while the mom was still living. On the phone, I asked if the attorney was planning to gift the mom's assets to the daughters while she was still living.

The attorney replied, "No, no, no. I am not gifting those assets! We're naming the four daughters as beneficiaries so they can get the step-up in basis."

It turned out to be a simple misunderstanding. Our client did not understand what her attorney planned to do. We did the right thing by reaching out to the attorney, being a team player, and making sure everybody was acting in the family's best interests. Even though the other three sisters were not working with us at the time, we still wanted to make sure everything was being done right—not only for the daughter we represent, but for the entire family.

If we had acted on that misunderstanding without confirming it, it would have been costly for the four sisters. Proactive communication among everyone involved is a must when making important decisions like this.

Proactive communication among everyone involved is a must when making important decisions

Why Roth IRA Conversions Are Common

We work with quite a few families on Roth conversions.

A key difference between a Roth IRA and a traditional IRA is that with a Roth IRA, your money grows tax-free, and you can typically make tax- and penalty-free withdrawals after the age of 59½. With a traditional IRA, you contribute pre- or after-tax dollars, your money grows tax-deferred, and withdrawals are taxed as current income after the age of 59½.

A *Roth IRA conversion* involves transferring retirement funds from a traditional IRA, a simplified employee pension (SEP), or a SIMPLE IRA, or from a defined-contribution plan such as a 401(k), into a Roth IRA. As the account owner, you will have to pay income tax on the money you convert; however, you will then be eligible to make tax-free withdrawals from the account in the future. If you believe you will move into a higher tax bracket in the future, you can save money by paying taxes now rather than later.

Because Roth IRAs were not as prevalent 20 or 30 years ago as they are now, some of the older folks we work with are not aware of them.

One of the people we serve is a retired firefighter with the Fire Department of New York (FDNY); he is only in his early fifties. Between his pension and his current income, he has more money coming in now, in retirement, than he did when he was working full-time. Over his career, he built up about $1 million in traditional retirement assets.

When he has to start taking money out of those accounts, to comply with federal required minimum distributions (RMDs), that money will be taxable to him. We are working with him to convert as much of his $1 million in retirement savings as we can before he reaches that point, moving that money out of his traditional accounts and into a Roth IRA. We are working with his accountant to do that in a very tax-efficient manner.

He won't necessarily *need* to take money out of those accounts to live on, but the government will require him to withdraw the money. He has more income now than he knows what to do with. His view is, "I want to handle this in the smartest way possible. I want to pay the taxes on the money now and ensure that neither I nor my beneficiaries will ever have to pay taxes on it again." So he's going to take the tax hit now.

You can see how it can require very complicated planning, strategy, and coordination to manage taxes on your money effectively. We have to consider the tax implications of every move, both now and in the future.

Market Fluctuations Affect Your Taxes, Too

Just as tax rates fluctuate and change people's situations, fluctuations in the stock and bond markets create changes as well. For example, if the markets go down, a family might face a lesser tax liability.

When markets declined toward the end of 2022, it created an interesting opportunity.

For example, if a family had $100,000 in an IRA at the beginning of 2022 and wanted to convert the entire amount to Roth, they would have had to pay taxes on $100,000, and then that money would have grown tax-free in perpetuity. But with the market decline, that same $100,000 was worth less than it was—let's say $75,000. So if they converted it later, their tax liability would be significantly less because their asset was worth $25,000 less than it had been.

If they converted that money to Roth, any growth from that point on would be tax-free. So, assuming the markets go back up again in the near future, it's almost like they're converting $100,000 worth of assets for only $75,000 worth of tax today.

Again, a fluctuation in investments typically affects taxes, and vice versa, so it will affect your decision making. Please work with your fiduciary advisor to make decisions about taking gains or losses in specific accounts, based on what the markets have done in that given year.

The Value of Exploring Various "What If?" Scenarios

When we are building a personal financial plan, many questions arise. Given the facts we know now and those we don't, we could end up with many different scenarios and outcomes. It's difficult to calculate these scenarios effectively and efficiently on our own: "Hey, if I do this, what would my tax liability be?" Every level of income and every different kind of transaction can produce a different tax impact.

The tools we use make it easy for us to model what those taxes will look like based on different financial decisions. When we explore those various scenarios, we typically share them with a client's CPA as well because again, we are not qualified to give tax advice. We simply want to illustrate for our clients how certain decisions could impact them from a tax perspective. Running these scenarios makes it a lot easier for them to visualize the outcomes.

> **The tools we use make it easy for us to model what those taxes will look like based on different financial decisions.**

Running these different scenarios was helpful for the retired firefighter I mentioned earlier. We explored some hypothetical situations, showing him how his tax liability would change from last year if he did a $50,000 Roth conversion versus a $100,000 conversion.

The more clearly you understand the potential tax

impact of various financial decisions, the easier it will be for you to make well-informed decisions that will benefit you the most. Also, the stronger the partnership between your CPA and your fiduciary advisor is, the more they can optimize your tax strategy and family's financial future.

Exchange-Traded Funds (ETFs) vs. Mutual Funds

When working with families, we typically use exchange-traded funds (ETFs) and individual securities a lot more than mutual funds. For one reason, mutual funds have a tendency to distribute capital gains and are more expensive to own.

ETFs were first introduced in 1993, and they have grown steadily over the years, now comprising more than $10 trillion in investor assets globally. In the United States, the ETF market exceeds $5 trillion, roughly one-quarter the size of the US mutual fund market.[45]

Many investors like ETFs because they combine features of mutual funds and stocks, often at a lower

---

45. "Tackling ETFs: What You Should Know," Motley Fool Wealth Management, last updated August 10, 2022, https://foolwealth.com/insights/tackling-etfs-what-you-should-know?utm_source=google&utm_medium=cpc&utm_campaign=-Search_MF_Evergreen_InsightsBlogLP&utm_term=an%20etf&utm_content=&gclid=Cj0KCQjwqoibBhDUARIsAH2Op-WhIyKzFj-vlm7vhztqTs6BXB2BdgTfLQHFKsVOfqoQf8D-FlK3YSBS0aAkQpEALw_wcB.

cost. Like a mutual fund, an ETF is a bundle of many securities that you can buy in one purchase, giving investors the potential benefit of diversification. Like stocks, ETFs are traded all day on an exchange and can be bought any time during the day for their trading price at that moment. In contrast, mutual funds can be bought only after the trading day ends, when their price for the day—the Net Asset Value, or NAV—is calculated. (You can place an order for a mutual fund during the day, but it won't be executed until the end of trading.) Like stocks and mutual funds, there are many types of ETFs.[46]

Now, typically, if you have ETFs and individual securities, the only time you are going to incur a capital gain, for the most part, is when you sell a security you own. But mutual funds often distribute capital gains. We have seen instances in which families have owned mutual funds, their mutual funds were down for the year, and they had to pay a tax bill because a capital gain was distributed.

Mutual funds, on the other hand, are run by professional money managers who decide which securities to buy (stocks, bonds, etc.) and when to sell them. You get exposure to all the investments in the fund and any income they generate. Most mutual funds fall into one of four main categories: money market

---

46. Ibid.

funds, bond funds, stock funds, and target date funds. Each type has different features, risks, and rewards.

These products can seem complicated, so please consult with your fiduciary advisor.

Again, my goal in sharing this information with you is not to offer a comprehensive look at the many types of financial products; I simply want to widen awareness about how every potential decision you make can affect your financial situation. The more you know, the better chance you have of optimizing your financial outcome.

Many times, people in the higher tax brackets are better off being in individual securities and ETFs than in mutual funds.

Families need to be aware of how various products work, as well as when they are and are not the best choice. Many times, people in the higher tax brackets are better off being in individual securities and ETFs than in mutual funds.

If you are in mutual fund, you have to understand what the tax cost is going to be and how that will affect your investment over time.

Just be aware, and be careful of capital gains distributions. You could end up paying a very large tax bill with little or no gain, or even loss of principal. You have to be mindful of the effect of taxes on the investment itself, how you're being taxed, and when those distributions will take place. You might want to time your investment differently, based on when the distribution is being made.

This is an just one of many important details that gets overlooked more often than not, often at significant cost.

Can Do-It-Yourselfers Manage Their Tax Burden Effectively?

Could a do-it-yourselfer get the same results, without working with a fiduciary advisor?

Possibly. But that person would need to have a lot of knowledge about how all these components are related. He or she also would have to keep up with changing rules and regulations.

In my experience, when people attempt to DIY their financial and tax planning, a lot of details fall through the cracks for those folks. We have also seen people run into problems when they try to do the planning on their own or when they have financial advisors who are not proactive about planning and fail to evaluate and adjust their plans plan over time.

This is why we pride ourselves on our proactive communication and teamwork among professionals with different expertise to make sure we're doing what's in every family's best interest along the way.

Chapter 9—Making It Personal

1. I strongly encourage you to work with your fiduciary financial advisor and tax professionals to ensure that your tax liability is being managed well. One mistake, or even one misunderstanding, can be costly to you and, in some cases, irreversible.
2. Please don't allow the complexity of some tax issues to discourage you from educating yourself about key issues. Rely on your fiduciary advisor to guide you.
3. In general, aim to keep as much of your money as you can so you can pursue whatever brings you the most joy in life!
4. Recognize that everyone has to pay taxes and that every financial decision you make carries with it some type of tax-related implication.
5. What did you do today that brought you joy?*

The Value of a Fiduciary Advisor

In the previous nine chapters, I discussed some of the most important aspects of financial planning:

1. Discovering your "why"/purpose
2. Paying yourself first
3. Using a side hustle to reach your goals
4. Determining how much money you might need to sustain your lifestyle during retirement
5. Planning for retirement
6. Budgeting your money to stay on track with your plan
7. Saving early for college for your children and/or grandchildren
8. Protecting your assets and income
9. Navigating the tax consequences of every financial decision

Each one of these aspects of financial planning is critical to your financial future (if it applies to you) and requires careful consideration. Each aspect can be somewhat complex on its own, and when combined, the entire financial-planning process can seem intimidating and overwhelming.

This is why, in every chapter, I have recommended that you work with a *fiduciary* advisor.

As I mentioned in chapter 1, a *fiduciary financial advisor* is one who is obligated by law to act in your best interests as he or she manages your money and other assets. Instead of recommending products to you that will net the advisor a higher fee or commission, a *fiduciary* advisor is obligated to make recommendations that benefit you, the customer.

Because financial planning can seem overwhelming at times, it can increase your confidence about your situation if you work closely with a fiduciary financial advisor to develop your personal financial plan and adjust it as needed over time. He or she will always work with your best interests in mind.

> **A *fiduciary financial advisor* is one who is obligated by law to act in your best interests as he or she manages your money and other assets.**

Working with an advisor who is held to the highest standard of professionalism can relieve you of the stress, uncertainty, and worry associated with not knowing where you stand financially. Turning that important aspect of your well-being over to an expert frees up your time and energy to derive more joy from the things you enjoy in life.

You might see the term "registered investment advisor (RIA)" when searching for an advisor. An RIA is a firm that advises clients on securities investments and may manage their investment portfolios. RIAs are registered with either the US Securities and Exchange Commission (SEC) or state securities administrators. RIAs have fiduciary obligations to their clients, meaning that they have a fundamental duty to always and only provide investment advice that is in their clients' best interests.

Please note that this fiduciary standard applies only to investment advisors. It does not apply to advisors who sell insurance products, for example, or financial planners who provide planning services but who do not manage your investments.

Know the Difference Between a Broker and a Fiduciary

There are two main categories of financial advisors: brokers and fiduciaries. Let's look at how they differ.

1. Brokers

A *broker* is FINRA-licensed and has a Series 7 certification. Those are the credentials that brokers are required to have, but I think the more important piece is their level of responsibility to you as a client.

FINRA requires that brokers know each client and

then recommend products and services that align with that client's needs. This is called "client suitability," and it is part of a FINRA mandate called the "Know Your Customer" rule.[47]

They have to know you as a person and understand your unique situation and needs. As long as they make recommendations that they feel are appropriate for you, then they've satisfied their due diligence. Typically, brokers are compensated via commission. For example, if your advisor recommends that you buy a mutual fund as an investment and you do so, then the broker will get a commission for that sale. Then your broker might buy stocks for you—let's say shares in IBM stock. You pay the broker a commission for that purchase. This is the scenario I mentioned in chapter 1, in which the broker got paid every time he made a trade.

Brokers' required level of responsibility to you is that they have to *know you as a customer*—that's it. The law does not mandate that they act in your best interest.

2. Fiduciaries

A *fiduciary* has a much higher level of responsibility than a broker—to always act in their clients' best interests. This is much different from the broker's responsibility to simply know his or her clients.

---

47. "FINRA Rules: 2090. Know Your Customer," Financial Industry Regulatory Authority (FINRA), https://www.finra.org/rules-guid-ance/rulebooks/finra-rules/2090.

I realize this difference between brokers and fiduciaries might sound like semantics. But we're not just talking about a few differences in words or definitions. There is a significant difference between brokers just being required to know their customers and fiduciaries being required to always act in their clients' best interests.

Now, some advisors are both brokers and fiduciaries. They work with clients in a brokerage capacity and are compensated as brokers under the FINRA "Know Your Customer" rule. At the same time, they can also open investment accounts and work with families in the role of a fiduciary.

Often, people do not realize that advisors who operate in both roles sometimes have their broker hat on and sometimes have their fiduciary hat on.

Often, people do not realize that advisors who operate in both roles sometimes have their broker hat on and sometimes have their fiduciary hat on.

It's a very fine line, but it is important to know whether your advisor is acting as a fiduciary *all the time.*

This is why I always make this recommendation to the families we serve. As you interview advisors to find one who is a good fit for you and your situation, ask each one, "Are you a fiduciary?" An advisor who cannot answer this simple question with a definitive, confident "Yes" might not be your best option.

If the advisor says, "Yes, I am a fiduciary," then I recommend taking that one step further by asking, "Are you a fiduciary *all the time?*"

This is one of those important details that gets lost in the jargon and the not-straightforward English that's often used in our profession. But it is important to know this!

As I've recommended throughout this entire book, *work with a fiduciary advisor*. And make sure he or she is a fiduciary all the time.

One of the people we work with wrote the following review for us, and it appears on our Mitlin Financial website:[48]

> I have been a client of Mitlin Financial since 2011 and would highly recommend their services. Larry and his team deliver truly professional financial planning services and put their clients' interests first. I did not really understand the role of a fiduciary until I worked with Larry. He

---

48. Via Larry Sprung's LinkedIn page, by John C. CWM, LLC, and/or the financial professional received the testimonial(s) appearing herein from a verified client. The testimonial(s) reflect(s) the real-life experiences of individuals who used our services. However, CWM, LLC, and the financial professional do not claim, nor should the reader assume, that any individual experience recounted is typical or representative of what any other client might experience. The testimonial(s) displayed include(s) the original wording of the writer, except for grammatical, spelling, and typing edits. All reviews and testimonials are reviewed for authenticity prior to use.

works with integrity and provides sound financial advice and guidance. Mitlin has assisted me with some complex financial issues, and I have been more than happy with the results. So much so that I have entrusted Larry to guide all three of my kids as they enter their careers and life in their 20s. Larry is a pleasure to deal with, and I have no hesitation in recommending Mitlin's services with complete trust.

I include this quote here to point out that often, people do not understand the distinction between a fiduciary and a broker, even if they have worked with other advisors before coming to us. I think it is paramount to understand the difference and to make sure you are working with a fiduciary. It can make a tremendous difference over time.

It has never made sense to me why people would work with somebody who is not a fiduciary working in their best interests. And a broader conversation that goes well beyond the scope of this book is that I don't understand how in this day and age, anybody could be an advisor—advising people on critical decisions about their finances, wealth, and future— without being a fiduciary.

It has never made sense to me why people would work with somebody who is not a fiduciary working in their best interests.

Other Professions Set High Standards, Too

Any professional you work with is a fiduciary—or should be.

If you want to hire a skilled mechanic to repair your vehicle, you might seek out a mechanic who is ASE-certified. This means the mechanic has passed stringent requirements and exams that the Automotive Service Excellence organization manages.

When looking to hire an accountant, you can hire one who is a Certified Public Accountant (CPA). The CPA designation distinguishes licensed accounting professionals who are committed to protecting the public interest. To earn the CPA license, accounting professionals must have extensive education—at least 150 hours—pass a rigorous four-part exam and meet experience requirements. They must also commit to lifelong learning and adhere to a strict Code of Professional Conduct that requires competence, objectivity, integrity, and independence.[49]

And if you want to hire a surgeon who has been vetted professionally, you will probably seek out a board-certified surgeon who has met high professional standards. Once a physician has completed medical

---

49. "Certified Public Accountant," AICPA & CIMA, https://www.aicpa-cima.com/designations-certifications/certified-public-accountant-cpa.html.

school and the required number of years of accredited medical or surgical postgraduate training, he or she must take written and oral examinations to verify knowledge and competency to become board-certified.

These are all important services we all seek from professionals. You want to make sure you are hiring experts who not only have met stringent requirements but also those who will always act in your best interests.

This is just as important when seeking out a professional financial advisor to guide you through all aspects of personal financial planning.

How to Know if an Advisor Is a Fiduciary

As of September 2022, there were close to 204,000 finance advisors in the United States.[50] But not every financial advisor is a fiduciary. So, how can you determine which advisors are fiduciaries?

Here are three simple ways to find out if a financial advisor is a fiduciary.

1. **Ask the question.** As I mentioned, one way to find out if an advisor is a fiduciary is to *ask* him or her that question. If they cannot answer with a confident "Yes," then chances are, the

---

50. "Finance Advisor Demographics and Statistics in the US," Zippia, https://www.zippia.com/finance-advisor-jobs/demographics/.

advisor is not a fiduciary. And again, if the advisor says he or she is a fiduciary, be sure to ask the important follow-up question, "Are you a fiduciary *all the time*?"

2. **Work with an advisor who is a CERTIFIED FINANCIAL PLANNER**™. The CFP® certification is the standard of excellence in financial planning. CFP® professionals meet rigorous education, training, and ethical standards, and they are committed to serving their clients' best interests. Anyone who holds the CFP® certification is a fiduciary.

3. **Find out how the advisor is paid.** Another indication that an advisor is a fiduciary is that he or she is paid separately for building your personal financial plan on a "fee for service" basis and for managing your investments. Most fiduciaries obtain either 100 percent of their revenue from fees for services or from fees paid directly to them by clients and insurance commissions. Advisors who are receiving commissions from mutual funds and stock transactions typically are not fiduciaries.

Ask Questions if You Don't Understand an Advisor's Recommendation

I don't know of any advisors who have violated their fiduciary obligations to clients, but it can happen.

If you ever feel uncomfortable about a recommendation an advisor is making to you, I encourage you to speak up and find out why he or she is making that recommendation. Don't worry about offending the advisor; your primary goal is to protect your family. If an advisor seems to become defensive when you ask questions, I think that tells you a lot right there.

It is in everyone's best interest for clients to understand our recommendations. Let's say you and I were working together and you said to me, "Hey, I appreciate this recommendation,

> **It is in everyone's best interest for clients to understand our recommendations.**

but why do you think it's a good idea? What's the benefit to me?" If I know you as a person and understand your unique needs and goals, it should be easy for me to describe the benefits of my recommendation. If an advisor seems to have a difficult time explaining a recommendation, that can be a telling sign that he or she might be more interested in the advisor compensation involved than about your best interests.

I don't think any advisor who's been practicing

for a good period of time, who has a good reputation, and who acts as a fiduciary would have any issue with a family asking further questions about something. Typically, those questions arise when an advisor hasn't done a good job of explaining a recommendation and how it will benefit the client.

Sometimes, an advisor might make an appropriate recommendation, but you prefer not to move forward on it, for whatever reason. It is your choice and your right to tell your advisor you do not wish to move forward with the recommendation.

Here is one example of how that played out with a family we work with. About seven years ago, we presented to a family the idea of long-term care. At the time, they had three children who were all either in college or getting ready to enroll. The family had a lot of expenses to focus on, and long-term care was one of the few elements that was missing from their personal financial plan. We stressed to them the importance of protecting their financial future against the possibility of either spouse needing long-term medical care.

We presented it as an option, but unfortunately, and against our advice, they decided to punt on it at that time and not move forward with it. Fast-forward seven years later—we've been talking about long-term care with this family again. We bring up the topic every couple of years because we feel it is in their best interest to get long-term-care insurance in place. Now, even though I believe this coverage is in their best interest, it would not be in their best interest for me to *push* them into purchasing long-term-care insurance. My recommendation is in their best interest, but if I force them into something they're not ready to do, then I don't think that is in their best interest.

By now, this couple's children have all graduated from college, so they no longer have those college expenses they once had. And interestingly, both spouses' parents are having health issues, which is causing them to look into potential long-term-care needs for them. This recommendation makes more sense to this family now than it did seven years ago.

The point here is that just because an advisor makes a recommendation at a particular time, it doesn't mean you have to act on it right then—even if doing so might benefit you. If you can't fit the coverage into your budget, it makes no sense for you to create a financial hardship to try to fit it in.

There is significant value in developing a long-term professional relationship with a fiduciary advisor.

There is significant value in developing a long-term professional relationship with a fiduciary advisor. Knowing you and your situation well, he or she can easily adjust your personal financial plan as needed, over time.

More About How Advisors Are Paid

There was a time when people worked with financial advisors on a *transactional* basis—when they needed to purchase stocks, bonds, or mutual funds, for example. But today, the profession is moving away from transactional relationships and toward long-term, ongoing advice relationships.

McKinsey & Company, a global management consulting firm that was founded in 1926, attests to the bright future for our profession. In 2020, McKinsey published a report predicting what wealth management will look like in North America in 2030. The report predicts that in the financial services profession, a focus on asset management is giving way to a focus on financial advice:

> In the next ten years, advisors will gradually shed their role as investment managers and become more like integrated life/wealth coaches who advise clients on investments, banking, health care, protection, taxes, estate, and financial wellness needs more broadly. By 2030, at least 80 percent of advisors will offer goal-based advice, and about half of clients will actively pursue and track bite-sized goals (such as saving for three

college credits a month)—and this granular goal tracking will span customers' investment, protection, education, retirement, and broader wellness.

I agree that ongoing advice is the future of our profession, and this type of client–advisor relationship goes a long way toward keeping you on track to reach your goals as you navigate various life stages and circumstances. I don't know why any family would want to pay for simply a transactional relationship with an advisor when they could receive ongoing advice and guidance.

Three Scenarios That Demonstrate Why I Derive Joy from My Work

I want to conclude this book with three stories about families we serve that demonstrate why I derive so much joy from my role as a fiduciary financial advisor. It energizes me to know that our team at Mitlin has had a positive impact in the lives of the families we serve.

1. Guiding Two Generations to Develop a Plan and Work Toward Financial Success

Throughout the past ten years, we have worked with a family and have helped them navigate every aspect of their financial life. We helped them connect with the accounting firm, the estate-planning firm, and the life insurance provider they are working with currently.

After working with the husband and wife for a while, we then began working with their three adult children on an individual basis, with a focus on working toward financial success.

A couple of years ago, the husband said to me, "Mitlin has assisted me with some complex financial issues, and I have been more than happy with the results. So much so that I have entrusted Larry to guide all three of my kids as they enter their careers and life in their 20s. Larry is a pleasure to deal with, and I have no hesitation in recommending Mitlin's services with complete trust."[51]

It is incredibly rewarding to know we are making a difference in people's lives. It reinforces why we do what we do and why we love doing what we do every day.

---

51. Via Larry Sprung's LinkedIn page, by John C. CWM, LLC, and/ or the financial professional received the testimonial(s) appearing herein from a verified client. The testimonial(s) reflect(s) the real-life experiences of individuals who used our services. However, CWM, LLC, and the financial professional do not claim, nor should the reader assume, that any individual experience recounted is typical or representative of what any other client might experience. The testimonial(s) displayed include(s) the original wording of the writer, except for grammatical, spelling, and typing edits. All reviews and testimonials are reviewed for authenticity prior to use.

2. Prior Planning Helps to Minimize the Impact of a Critical Financial Event

Another couple we worked with were about a year and a half away from retirement. We developed a financial plan for the husband and wife. We were on track to successfully start executing that financial plan. As we began to implement it, we were looking to start moving them from the investment phase to the retirement phase. Unfortunately, about three months before this was supposed to happen, the husband had a major stroke, which could have derailed their plans, had they not been prepared. (I mentioned this client briefly in chapter 5.)

The thing that really helped this family was that they knew we had a very good understanding of their entire personal and financial picture. That enabled them to focus on the husband's healing process and to make sure he got the care, resources, and support he needed to recover from the stroke. Because we had a vast understanding of their financial situation, they felt more confident about that while the husband was sick.

This family's situation resonated with me because it reminds me of my parents' situation. I talk about often how my mom's illness shaped my "why"—my compelling purpose for guiding others as a fiduciary financial advisor. When my mom was extremely ill and my dad was taking care of her, he did not have the type of support we lent to this family. I feel that he really would have benefited from it.

Having the support and guidance of a financial advisor would not have mitigated my mom's illness, as I have mentioned, but I think it would have made my dad's life a heck of a lot easier if he had somebody to help navigate the situation. If he didn't have to worry about the financial aspects of the situation as much, he could have focused just on taking care of my mom.

Because our team has a really good understanding of this family's situation, from working with them closely, it has allowed them to focus on the husband's care and health. We have made some changes to their overall financial plan. They have always felt confident that they could do what they wanted and needed to do because of the work we had done leading up to this life-altering situation.

I'm happy to report that the husband has had a tremendous rebound. He is probably 98 percent back to his previous physical condition. He is doing rehab and improving. Of course this family's goals and objectives have changed moving forward, but all in all, we were able to successfully navigate them through this critical financial event with relative ease.

There is no substitute for being prepared and getting your personal financial plan established as early as possible.

3. Building a Professional Team to Guide a Family-Owned Business

A family we worked with owned and operated their own business, and they were in a great financial position. The business started to grow exponentially. Like most business owners, the family was focused on the operation and growth of the business. They worked with a local accountant who was very capable at handling the basic needs of regular W-2 employees, but he was not skilled enough to work with a business of their size and scope.

We worked with the family to get the right accounting partner, the right estate-planning attorney, and the right planning. We worked as a team to address all the areas of their financial life outside the business so that they didn't have to focus on those important aspects of their financial life. As a result, they were able to concentrate on the growth of the business. We are helping them in that area as well, introducing them to key partners who can help them grow the business further.

This family told us they believe their business experienced its tremendous growth largely because they were working with us. Hearing that kind of positive feedback is incredibly rewarding, and it reinforces the value of working with a team of experts who are committed to a family's success.

It is my honor to serve, and I am thrilled that, after years of thinking about writing a book, I was finally able to share my story and the Mitlin team's passion. I am so excited about our growth and look forward to meeting and serving new families. It is such an exciting time in our profession, as technology, financial psychology, and the ease of communication allow us to make planning more personal than ever.

Thank you for reading *Financial Planning Made Personal*! If you learned even one helpful strategy, concept, or idea from this book, then I consider it to be a success. I encourage you to reach out to me or anyone else at Mitlin Financial as you plan your future. In any event, I encourage you to spend your time, effort, and energy pursuing all the things in life that bring you joy.

Chapter 10—Making It Personal

1. If you do not have a fiduciary financial advisor yet, I strongly recommend that you find one to work with. If you do have a financial advisor, ask if he or she is a fiduciary. If not, then consider shopping around for one who is. I strongly advise that you work with a fiduciary financial advisor.
2. If you are working with a financial advisor and he or she makes a recommendation, and you do

not understand how it benefits you, ask a lot of questions until you do understand the benefits.

3. If an advisor makes a recommendation to you, but you do not feel the time is right to take that action, do not allow the advisor to pressure you into doing so. Acting in your best interests means making appropriate recommendations; it also means understanding if you cannot or do not want to pursue a recommendation at any given time.

4. When working with professionals in any profession—not just financial advisors—expect that they will act in your best interests. If they do not, find someone who will. Ensuring you are receiving the highest possible level of service in any area of your life will help you maintain the highest possible level of joy!

5. What did you do today that brought you joy?*

About the Author

Lawrence D. (Larry) Sprung, CFP®
Wealth Advisor and Founder
Mitlin Financial, Inc.
lsprung@mitlinfinancial.com
(631) 952-4466, x111
www.mitlinfinancial.com

With unwavering commitment to financial literacy, diversity, unparalleled client service, and humility, Larry Sprung founded Mitlin Financial, Inc., in 2004. He and his team consistently help the families they serve make healthy financial decisions and offer a tremendous experience that leverages personal service with today's top tools and technology.

Mitlin Financial is named in memory of Larry's wife's grandfather, Mitchell, and his mother, Linda. His mom is more than just the "lin" in Mitlin—she is the reason Larry does what he does. As a teen, he watched his parents struggle with their finances as his mom battled breast cancer for more than a decade. This became the driving force that led him on his journey to founding Mitlin Financial.

He was also inspired by the story of Mitchell,

though he never met him. He heard countless stories about his wife's grandfather's giving nature and willingness to lend an open ear. When Larry was forming Mitlin Financial, he thought a lot about these two people who, remarkably, passed away within hours of each other. He feels that they embody so many of the qualities Larry wants his firm to embody.

You can hear more of the Mitlin story in Episode 1 of the Mitlin Money Mindset™, which Larry hosts. You can find the Mitlin Money Mindset™ podcast on most major podcast platforms. Find it on your favorite platform to listen and subscribe.

During his more than 20 years in financial services, Larry has found that a lot of industry terms and concepts can seem confusing to outsiders. That's why he works with the families he serves to break down complex financial topics into easy-to-understand concepts. He wants to make sure they understand the tailored financial plan that is being laid out for them.

Today, Larry leads the planning and asset-management services at Mitlin, in addition to focusing on business development. He is also committed to offering educational workshops, in which he shares his knowledge and insights on a diverse set of financial topics. He is a frequent speaker at industry conferences and regularly films the firm's "Mitlin Minute" videos that provide important information on relevant financial topics.

Larry earned a bachelor's degree in mathematics from Binghamton University before entering the financial services industry in 1996. Helping the families he serves to pursue—and even set higher-reaching—financial goals continuously inspires and energizes him. He is proud to serve the second and third generations of families he serves. He has seen firsthand how strong financial habits instilled in parents, children and grandchildren can impact a family's wealth and wealth stewardship for generations.

In recognition of Larry's significant contributions to his profession, he has received recognition from quite a few professional organizations. He is honored to have been recognized by ThinkAdvisor as a LUMINARIES 2022 Finalists in the Thought Leadership Individuals Category. The award acknowledges Larry's commitment to financial literacy.

In 2021, Larry was named to the Investopedia 100 Top Advisors in 2021 and even more humbled to make their Top Ten list for 2022. He considers it a true honor to be on this list with so many professionals who are working to make an impact in the financial services profession.

In 2019, he was named a finalist for the Invest in Others for Community Service Award for his work in the mental-health space. He was also included on the *Long Island Business News* "40 Under 40" list, which recognizes distinguished professionals who give back to the community.

Giving back to his profession and community is one of Larry's greatest passions. He is especially committed to raising awareness for mental health. For more than 12 years, he served on the National Board of the American Foundation for Suicide Prevention, and he sits on its financial and investment committees. He and his wife, Denise, have raised more than $1.7 million for the organization through the Keith Milano Memorial Fund. The fund was created at AFSP in memory of Larry's brother-in-law.

Larry is donating the net proceeds from sales of this book to the Keith Milano Memorial Fund.

In addition, Larry volunteers through Family Reach, providing *pro bono* financial-planning services to those dealing with a cancer diagnosis.

Serious hockey Dad.

He values his family tremendously, and his desire to do right by his wife and sons drives who he is, both in and out of the office. You'll likely find Larry and his family at any number of ice hockey events on a given weekend.

Larry loves hockey so much, in fact, that his team at Mitlin Financial began a social media trend of posting the question "Which rink is Larry at?" We would select a winner from among those who guessed correctly and tagged a charity, and we would donate $100 to that charity.

How We Help

The services listed below are some of the key areas in which Mitlin Financial serves families with care, compassion, and honesty every step of the way:

- **Financial planning**—Our team of financial planning professionals will design a plan that evaluates your current situation by analyzing your assets, income, and expenditures to identify what assets you need today and what you can do to pursue your financial goals (the "big picture"). We provide regular reviews and modifications, ensuring that your financial plan stays current and dynamic.
- **Investment management**—As fiduciary advisors, we always act in your best interests. When you become a client of ours, our interests are immediately aligned with yours. That means we offer you only the strategies, solutions, or products we think will work in your best interest and will guide you toward your financial goals. We leverage a disciplined investment process to provide you with transparency of information, seamless proactive service, and the trust and accountability you need to pursue your

financial objectives. Combining the latest technology with the expertise of our team of financial professionals, we regularly monitor your portfolio to ensure it reflects your financial goals, even in the midst of unexpected changes in your circumstances.

- **Retirement planning**—We guide you toward, into, and through retirement by using our five-step process to build your personal financial plan.
- **Tax planning**—Working with our team of tax professionals, we will assess the tax consequences of every potential financial decision you make and recommend what we believe is your best course of action.
- **Insurance planning**—Protecting your financial future is one of the most important aspects of any personal financial plan. We work with our network of experts to ensure you have appropriate coverage for your unique needs.
- **Education funding**—Whether you establish a 529 plan or another method of saving for your children's and/or grandchildren's education, we will build this priority into your personal financial plan.
- **Financial guidance for book authors and other literary professionals**—We will transform your creative successes into solid

financial footing. We will coordinate with our trusted team of legal and accounting professionals to address your needs and to guide you toward your financial goals.

Please contact our office for a no-obligation consultation to discover if we are a good fit for each other:

Mitlin Financial
https://www.mitlinfinancial.com/
(631) 952-4466
140 Adams Ave., Ste. B-12
Hauppauge, NY 11788

Disclosures

Investment advisory services offered through CWM, LLC, an SEC Registered Investment Advisor. Carson Partners, a division of CWM, LLC, is a nationwide partnership of advisors. The opinions expressed by Lawrence Sprung in Financial Planning Made Personal *are for general information only and are not intended to provide specific advice or recommendations for any individual.*

To determine what may be appropriate for you, consult with your attorney, accountant, and financial or tax advisor prior to investing. Investors should also consider whether the investor's or beneficiary's home state offers any state tax or other benefits available only from that state's 529 Plan. Any state-based benefit should be one of many appropriately weighted factors in making an investment decision. Investors should consult their financial or tax advisor before investment in any state's 529 Plan.

The hypothetical investment results are for illustrative purposes only and should not be deemed a representation of past or future results. Actual investment results may be more or less than those shown. This does not represent any specific product and/or service.

The charitable entities and/or fund-raising opportunities described herein are not endorsed by, or affiliated, with CWM, LLC, or its affiliates. Our philanthropic interests are personal to us and are not reviewed, sponsored, or approved by CWM, LLC.

Converting from a traditional IRA to a Roth IRA is a taxable event.

This document has been prepared by your advisor, is for informational purposes only, and does not replace the statements you should receive directly from your Custodian, the investment sponsor, or any other outside custodian. The information in this report has been prepared from data believed to be reliable, but no representation is being made as to its accuracy or completeness.

The RMD figures given here are representative only of the accounts shown. Your RMD figures may vary based on outside accounts not listed. For a comprehensive review of your personal situation, always consult with a tax or legal advisor. CWM, LLC, any other named entity, or any of their representatives may not give legal or tax advice.

A Roth IRA offers tax-free withdrawals on taxable contributions. To qualify for the tax-free and penalty-free withdrawal or earnings, a Roth IRA must be in place for at least five tax years, and the distribution must take place after age 59½ or due to death, disability, or a first-time home purchase (up to a $10,000 lifetime maximum). Depending on state law, Roth IRA distributions may be subject to state taxes.

The views stated in this book are not necessarily the opinion of CWM, LLC, and should not be construed directly or indirectly as an offer to buy or sell any securities mentioned herein. Due to volatility within the markets mentioned, opinions are subject to change with notice. Information is based on sources believed to be reliable; however, their accuracy or completeness cannot be guaranteed. Past performance does not guarantee future results.

CWM, LLC, and/or the financial professional received the testimonial(s) appearing herein from a verified client. The testimonial(s) reflect(s) the real-life experiences of individuals who used our services. However, CWM, LLC, and the financial professional do not claim, nor should the reader assume, that any individual experience recounted is typical or representative of what any other client might experience. The testimonial(s) displayed include(s) the original wording of the writer, except for grammatical, spelling, and typing edits. All reviews and *testimonials are reviewed for authenticity prior to use.*

ThinkAdvisor's 2022 Luminaries Award for Thought Leadership & Education awarded to Lawrence Sprung. Nominations are submitted on an application basis, and nominees are selected by a judging panel and editorial team based on the panel's assessment of the nominee's impact on their firm, its advisors, and the broader professional community and industry.

Investopedia 100 Top Financial Advisors (2021 & 2022): Awarded to Larry Sprung. Advisors who wished to be ranked self-submitted or peer-submitted answers to questions compiled by Investopedia. Rankings were determined based on the number of followers and engagement on social media, primary contribution to professional industry websites, and their focus on financial literacy. An advisor's ranking on this list does not ensure that a client or prospective client will experience a higher level of performance or results, nor a guarantee of future investment success.

www.ingramcontent.com/pod-product-compliance
Lightning Source LLC
Chambersburg PA
CBHW041915190326

41458CB00024B/6268